# Tobacco Talk

# Tobacco Talk

AND

# Smokers' Gossip

*An amusing Miscellany of Fact
and Anecdote relating to the "Great
Plant" in all its Forms and Uses
including a Selection from
Nicotian Literature*

**Fredonia Books
Amsterdam, The Netherlands**

Tobacco Talk and Smokers' Gossip

by
Anonymous Author

ISBN: 1-4101-0270-X

Reprinted from the 1884 edition

Fredonia Books
Amsterdam, The Netherlands
http://www.fredoniabooks.com

# On a Tobacco Jar.

Three hundred yeare ago or soe,
Ane worthye knight and gentlemanne
Did bring me here, to charm and chere
Ye physical and mental manne.
God rest his soule, who fild ye bowle,
And may our blessings finde him,
That he not misse some share of blisse
Who left soe much behind him!

Bernard Barker.

## PREFACE.

THE present collection of Notes and Anecdotes has been gleaned from the more generally interesting portion of a History of Tobacco, which for some few years has been in progress, and the materials for which were gathered from every available source.

Not only novels and plays, old newspapers, travels and memoirs, have been examined or perused; but the works of poets and satirists, histories, acts of parliament, technical treatises, the accounts of early voyages, collections of tracts and tobacco journals, have been ransacked for contributions on the use and abuse, the praise and blame, of the "plant divine."

For the delectation of all devotees of Tobacco; for those who take their Latakia from the seductive meerschaum, or Virginia from the clay; for those who taste the "naked beauties"

of sweet Havana, as well as those who
the "primrose path of dalliance tread"
with a cigarette between their teeth ;
we have brought together in this little
volume droll stories of the pipe, the
romantic history of the snuff-box,
odds and ends of Tobacco lore, and
pages of splendid panegyric by nico-
tians such as Charles Lamb and Byron,
Bulwer and Thackeray.

Here too will be found pleasant
gossip about famous tobacco-takers
from Raleigh to Tennyson ; not omit-
ting the small sins of royalty, the
backslidings of bishops (archbishops
too) in this respect ; soldiers and
doctors, lawyers and artists, poets and
peers—every one in short who is an
honour to nicotian society, among
whom one living lady at least must be
numbered—no less exalted a person-
age than an Empress !

The Editor desires to associate with
this work the name of a friend,
Mr. Ernest Darke, whose unremitting
labours augmented considerably the
mass of material from which *Tobacco
Talk* was derived.

# CONTENTS.

## Contents.

# INDEX.

# TOBACCO TALK

### AND

## SMOKER'S GOSSIP.

---

### A TOBACCO PARLIAMENT.

IT is a curious fact that Mary Stuart's son, James I., the fiercest foe of tobacco, should have been the ancestor of Friedrich Wilhelm I., the smoking King of Prussia, who founded the famous Tabaks-Collegium, which has made so much noise in the world. It was a sort of smoking club, "affording him," says Carlyle, "in a rough, natural way, the uses of a Parliament—a Parliament reduced to its simplest expression, and instead of parliamentary eloquence, provided with Dutch clay-pipes and tobacco." Tabagies were not uncommon among German sove-

A

reigns of that epoch. George I. at
Hanover had his smoking-room, and
select smoking party on an evening,
and even in London smoked nightly,
wetting his royal throat with thin beer.
Friedrich Wilhelm was a man of habitudes ;
his evening Tabagie became a law of nature to him, and finding that it would
serve in such a capacity, he turned it into
a political institution. A smoking-room,
with wooden furniture, was set apart in
each of his Majesty's royal palaces, for
this evening service, and became the Tabagie of his Majesty. Carlyle has described
in his picturesque manner, "a high large
room, contented saturnine human figures,
a dozen or so of them, sitting round a
large long table, furnished for the occasion, long Dutch pipe in the mouth of
each man, supplies of knaster easily ac-
cessible, small pan of burning peat, in the
Dutch fashion, is at your left hand ; at your
right a jug, which I find to consist of excellent thin bitter beer. Other costlier
materials for drinking, if you want such,
are not beyond reach. On side-tables
stand wholesome cold meats, royal rounds
of beef not wanting, with bread thinly sliced
and buttered : in a rustic but neat and
abundant way, such innocent accommoda-
tions, narcotic or nutritious, gaseous, fluid

and solid, as human nature, bent on con-
templation and an evening lounge, can re-
quire. Perfect equality is to be the rule,
no rising, or notice taken, when anybody
enters or leaves. Let the entering man
take his place and pipe, without obligatory
remarks; if he cannot smoke, which is
Seckendorf's case for instance, let him at
least affect to do so, and not ruffle the
established stream of things. And so,
Puff, slowly Pff!" Sometimes in this
large room, and oftener in the open air on
the steps of a fountain, the smoking ses-
sion was held. Seated, canvas-screened,
the King smoked there with select friends,
and chatted discursively till bedtime.

---

## NAPOLEON'S FIRST PIPE.

CONSTANT relates the following anecdote of the great NAPOLEON, who
once took a fancy to smoke, for the purpose
of trying a very fine Oriental pipe, which
had been presented to him by a Turkish
or Persian ambassador :

"Fire having been brought, it only remained to communicate it to the tobacco,
but that could never be effected by the
method which his Majesty adopted. He

contented himself with alternately opening and shutting his mouth, without at-
tempting to draw in his breath.    ' Oh,
the devil!' cried he at last, ' there will
be no end to this business.'    I observed
to him that he did it half-heartedly, and
showed him how he ought to begin.    But
the Emperor always returned to his yawn-
ing.    Wearied by his vain efforts, he at
last desired me to light the pipe.    I obeyed,
and gave it him.    But scarcely had he
drawn in a mouthful than the smoke,
which he knew not how to expel, turned
back into his palate, penetrated into his
throat, and came out by his nose and
blinded him.    As soon as he recovered
his breath, he ejaculated, ' Take that away
from me !    What abomination !    Oh, the
swine !—my stomach turns.'    In fact, he
felt himself so incommoded for at least an
hour, that he renounced for ever the pleasure of a habit which he said was only fit
to amuse sluggards."

---

A DUTCH POET AND NAPOLEON'S SNUFF-BOX.

IN April 1810, when Napoleon and Marie
    Louise visited the subterranean canal
of Saint Quentin and the towns of Cambrai.

Valenciennes, &c., the burgomaster of a little Dutch hamlet thought fit to add the following doggerel inscription to the triumphal arch that he had caused to be erected :—

> " Il n'a pas fait une sottise
> En épousant Marie Louise."

Napoleon no sooner saw this effusion, the effort of an imagination at once poetical and political, than he sent for the burgomaster. " M. le Maire," said he to him, " they cultivate the muses in your district ? " " Sire, I write a few verses now and then." " Ah ! you are, then, the author of the above couplet ? Do you take snuff?" added the Emperor, presenting him with a snuff-box enriched with diamonds. " Yes, sire, but I am quite overcome. . . ." " Help yourself, keep the box, and—

> " Quand vous y prendrez une prise
> Rappelez vous Marie Louise."

---

### FREDERICK THE GREAT AS AN ASS.

THE cynical temper of Frederick the Great is well known. He once made a present of a gold snuff-box to the brave Count Schwerin. Inside the lid the head of an ass had been painted. Next day, when dining with the King, Schwerin ostentatiously displayed his snuff-box. The King's sister, the Duchess of Brunswick, who happened to be staying at Potsdam, took it up and opened it. Immediately she exclaimed, "What a striking likeness! In truth, brother, this is one of the best portraits I have ever seen of you." Frederick, much embarrassed, thought that the Duchess was carrying the joke too far. She, however, passed the box to her neighbour, who gave vent to similar expressions of astonished admiration. The box made the round of the table, and every tongue waxed eloquent upon the subject of this "counterfeit presentment." The King was extremely puzzled, but when the box at length reached his own hands, he saw, to his great surprise and greater relief, that his portrait was indeed really there. The wily Count had simply employed an artist to remove with exceeding despatch the ass's head, and substitute for it the King's well-known features. His Majesty could not but laugh at the clever device which had so completely turned the tables on him.

## TOO SMALL FOR TWO.

FREDERICK THE GREAT took large quantities of snuff. To save himself the trouble of extracting it from his pocket, he had large snuff-boxes placed on each mantel-piece in his apartments, and from these would help himself as the fancy took him. One day he saw, from his study, one of his pages, believing himself unobserved, put his fingers unceremoniously into the open box on the adjoining mantel-piece. The King said nothing at the moment, but after the lapse of an hour he called the page, made him bring the snuff-box, and bidding the indiscreet youth take a pinch from it, said to him, "What do you think of the snuff?" "Excellent, sire." "And the box?" "Superb, sire." "Oh, well, sir, take it, for I think it is too small for both of us!"

## A SMOKING EMPRESS.

THE Empress of Austria is, perhaps, the only royal or imperial lady of the present age who may be regarded from a nicotian point of view with entire satisfac-

tion.   When at home she is generally very
tired, and having little taste for reading,
lolls back in a deep, soft, arm-chair, or lies
on a sofa, puffing cigarettes.   She has an al-
bum by her, with photographs of her horses,
her favourite dogs, her children, and her
grandchild.   She hates brilliant assemblies,
and thinks parliaments contemptible.   Very
capricious and strong-willed in carrying out
her whims, she can, in the German fashion,
put rank aside, and be very charming to
those who surround her, if such is her good
pleasure.   Captain Middleton, who is her
esquire in the hunting-fields of England
and Ireland, has never had a harsh word
from her Majesty.   With the circus-girl
Elise, who was a year or two ago the idol
of. the Parisian *boulevardiers*, her Majesty
is almost motherly.   The two smoke cigarettes, together, and talk gaily on equestrian
subjects—the only subjects, indeed, which
interest the Kaiserin.

---

### THE SMOKING PRINCESSES.

ALTHOUGH Louis XIV. had a great
dislike to tobacco, his daughters
were not above imitating some English
ladies of the period, and indulging in the

pipe. When the princesses grew weary
of the gravity and etiquette of the court
circle, relates Miss Pardoe, they were accustomed to celebrate a species of orgie in their
own apartments after supper; and on one
occasion, when the Dauphin had at a late
hour quitted the card-table, and hearing
a noise in their quarter of the palace,
entered to ascertain its cause, he found
his sisters engaged in smoking—some
say that they were at the same time
drinking brandy—and discovered that they
had borrowed their pipes from the officers
of the Swiss guard.

------------

## AN INCIDENT ON THE G. W. R.

THE scene was a first-class railway carriage. The date need not be mentioned. There were no ladies in the carriage. One of the passengers took out his
cigar-case, and, giving a look of inquiry, but
not making any remark, lit up, and vigorously puffed away. As he progressed towards the end of his cigar, he noticed a
look of great irritation on the face of his
*vis-à-vis.* " I am afraid, sir," said the
smoker, hurriedly, "that my cigar annoys
you?" "It does, sir; it annoys me exces-

sively." "I am sure I beg your pardon," said the gentleman, and threw his cigar out of the window. "That's all very well," said his fellow-passenger ; "but I mean to give you in charge directly I get to Bath. You were perfectly well aware that this is not a smoking carriage, and I mean to defend the rights of passengers." "I am really very sorry, sir; but I took it for granted that there was no objection." "I made up my mind, sir," was the dogmatic reproach, "soon after we left Swindon, that I would give you in charge on the first opportunity." Then there was an awkward pause, and presently the offender said, "Perhaps you will take my card? I happen to hold a public position, and should like to avoid any disturbance." "I don't want your card, sir." "But you had better look at it." The aggrieved passenger looked at it contemptuously, but it was the card of a royal duke ! Things now went on pleasantly; but before he left the carriage the gentleman awkwardly expressed a hope that H. R. H. would not think he had acted wrongly? "That is a point which we need not discuss," said H. R. H.

---

### RALEIGH'S TOBACCO-BOX.

SIR WALTER RALEIGH was no nig-
gard of his tobacco, if we may judge
from the size of his box.    In 1719 this relic
was preserved in the museum of Mr Ralph
Thoresby, of Leeds.   It was of cylindri-
cal form, about seven inches in diameter
and thirteen inches high ; the outside was
of gilt leather, and in the inside was a cavity
for a receiver of glass or metal, which
would hold about a pound of tobacco.   A
kind of collar, connecting the receiver
with the case, was pierced with holes for
pipes.

---

### BISMARCK'S LAST CIGAR.

GRANT and Bismarck, the one the
European, and the other the American "man of blood and iron," are equally
famous for their devotion to a good cigar.
No caricaturist who drew Grant without a
cigar in his mouth could hope to rise in his
profession.  Bismarck once told a group of
visitors the following story : " The value of
a good cigar," said he, proceeding to light
an excellent Havana, "is best understood

when it is the last you possess, and there is no chance of getting another.    At Königgrätz I had only one cigar left in my pocket, which I carefully guarded during the whole of the battle, as a miser guards his treasure.    I did not feel justified in using it.    I painted in glowing colours in my mind the happy hour when I should enjoy it after the victory.    But I had miscalculated my chances.    A poor dragoon lay helpless, with both arms crushed, murmuring for something to re-fresh him.    I felt in my pockets, and found that I had only gold, which would be of no use to him.    But stay—I had still my treasured cigar !    I lighted it for him, and placed it between his teeth.    You should have seen the poor fellow's grateful smile! I never enjoyed a cigar so much as that one which I did not smoke.

---

BISMARCK'S CIGAR STORY.

IN the memoirs of Dr. Moritz Busch, Bismarck's late secretary, may be found a characteristic anecdote showing how the Prussian statesman claimed and enforced his privilege of smoking at the sittings of the Military Commission of the

Diet at Frankfort.   The story is given in
the Chancellor's words :

"While Rochow represented Prussia at
the Diet, Count Rechberg, the president,
who represented Austria, was the only
member who smoked at the Board.
Rochow, who was a great smoker, often
longed to light a cigar, but did not dare.
When I arrived, however, I asked myself
why Prussia should not do as Austria did.
So at the first sitting I drew out a cigar
and asked Rechberg for a light, which he
gave me, stupefied at my coolness.   The
other delegates were not less amazed, and
wrote to their respective Governments for
instructions.   But the subject was a
serious one, requiring reflection, so six
months elapsed without their obtaining an
answer.   Meanwhile, Bothmer, the Hano-
verian, who was a great friend of Rechberg,
took the liberty of lighting up to be even
with me, seeing which, the Saxon, Nostitz,
produced a cigar to be equal with him.
There remained now only the delegates of
Wurtemberg and Darmstadt, but these two
were not smokers.   What was to be done?
Could they let their colleagues blow clouds
in their faces without blowing back?   The
Wurtemberger was the first to decide that
the honour of his country was involved,
and he brought out a cigar in his turn.   I

think I can see it now—an indefinable cigar, pale yellow, thin, tapering and enormously long.   He smoked it bravely, with all his might, and almost to the stump, thus giving a magnificent example of devotion to his country."

----

## MOLTKE'S POUND OF SNUFF.

THE successful strategist Count Moltke is an inveterate snuff-taker.   In the grand three weeks' campaign which culminated in that Prussian  " Waterloo," the battle of Sedan, his plans were assisted by a pound of snuff.   Throughout the Prussian advance, amid its tremendous anxieties, the General took snuff to excess, but at the supreme moment when the Uhlans announced  to him the march northwards of Marshal MacMahon, Moltke literally emptied his snuff-box as he entered his tent to organise the movement which resulted in the capture of Napoleon III. on the Belgian frontier.   And strange to tell, adds Mr. Steinmetz, Moltke was actually required, by the German War-Office, to pay for that memorable pound of snuff at the end of the war, when there was presented to him the bill (duly signed and  countersigned by various officials), which ran, " For one pound of snuff supplied to General Von Moltke, one thaler ! "

----

### LORD BROUGHAM AS A SMOKER.

WHEN Lord Brougham was in the zenith of his fame, he most certainly derived great benefit from a pipe. After having mystified a box of common jurymen in the Court of King's Bench, he took one pipe in the afternoon before proceeding to the House of Commons ; and after having spoken there for two or three hours, profusely mingling wit with wisdom, and instructing his opponents while he flayed them, he would return home to smoke another pipe, before quietly sitting down to an article for the *Edinburgh Review*. On the conclusion of the labours of the day, he took another pipe as a composer before going to bed. It has been said, however, that Brougham, from the time he donned his court suit at his first levee as Lord Chancellor, laid aside his pipe at once and for ever.

----

### MAZZINI'S SANG-FROID AS A SMOKER.

THIS famous Italian exile was fore-
warned that his assassination had
been planned and that men had been des-
patched to London for the purpose, but he
made no attempt to exclude them from his
house. One day the conspirators entered
his room and found him listlessly smoking.
" Take cigars, gentlemen," was his instant
invitation. Chatting and hesitation on
their part followed. " But you do not proceed to business, gentlemen," said Mazzini.
" I believe your intention is to kill me."
The astounded miscreants fell on their
knees, and at length departed with the
generous pardon accorded them, whilst a
longer puff of smoke than usual was the
only malediction sent after them.

Mazzini's last years in England were
spent at Old Brompton. The modest
chambers he occupied in Onslow-terrace
were strewed with papers and the tables
provided with cigars, that friends who
called might select their brands and join
him. He always kept a cigar burning
while he wrote. Canaries flew free about
the room. Lord Montairy, in " Lothair,"
smoked cigars so mild and delicate in
flavour that his wife never found him

out : Mazzini surely must have had some Montairy cigars, for his canaries did not find him out, or object to him if they did !

------

## LORD CLARENDON AS A SMOKER.

THE late Foreign Secretary was an inveterate smoker, and by his lamented decease in 1870, certain cigar-dealers lost an excellent customer. No man in Europe loved a good " weed " better than he. He used to smoke when attending to his official business, and the Foreign Office (while he was there) was always pervaded with a strong aroma of cigars. His despatches were generally written between midnight and daybreak, and during this time a cigar or cigarette scarcely ever left his lips. Lord Clarendon was never himself at a diplomatic conference till cigars were introduced. He and the late Emperor of the French had many a whiff together. Just after his death the newspapers had much to say of his love for the "weed." One journal had previously gone so far as to put these words in his mouth in a fancy sketch of a Cabinet Council meeting : " Diplomacy is entirely a question of the weed. I can always settle a quarrel if I know beforehand whether the plenipotentiary smokes Cavendish, Latakia or shag. ' Tobacco the key to diplomacy ' is my theme."

It was facetiously said that Murray would have given Lord Clarendon £20,000 for a work on the " Pipes, cigars, and tobaccos of all nations."

---

## POLITICS AND SNUFF-BOXES.

TALLEYRAND was a snuff-taker, not from devotion to the habit, but on principle. The wily politician used to say (and doubtless Metternich, who was a confirmed snuff-taker, would have agreed with him) that all diplomatists ought to take snuff, as it afforded a pretext for delaying a reply with which one might not be ready ; it sanctioned the removal of one's eyes from those of the questioner; occupied one's hands which might else convict one of nervous fidget ; and the action partly concealed that feature which is least easily schooled into hiding or belying human feelings —the mouth. If its workings were visible through the fingers, those twitches might be attributed to the agreeable irritation going on above.

No other article of *vertu* has been more extensively patronised by the crowned heads of Europe, for purposes of presentation, diplomatic or otherwise, than the snuff-box. In evidence of its importance as a means of keeping up friendly relations with foreign powers, we need only quote, from the account of sums expended at the coronation of George IV., the following entry :

Messrs. Randell and Bridge, for snuff-boxes to foreign ministers . . . £8,205 15 5

---

## PENN AND TOBACCO.

PENN abhorred tobacco. Whilst he was in America he was frequently annoyed by it. Once on his way to Pennsburgh he stopped at Burlington to see old friends, who happened to be smoking. Knowing his dislike to tobacco, they concealed their pipes. Perceiving from the smell when he entered the room that they had been smoking, he said pleasantly, "Well, friends, I am glad to see that you are at last ashamed of that vile habit." "Not so," replied Samuel Jennings, one of the company ; "but we

preferred laying down our pipes to offend-
ing a weak brother." It may have been
Penn's dislike to tobacco that caused the
old planters to enact that any master of a
vessel bringing a Quaker to Virginia should
be fined 5000 lb. of tobacco. But many
Quakers were quite free from their illustrious chief's prejudice.

---

### TOBACCO AND THE PAPACY.

IN 1642, Pope Urban VIII. promulgated
the following Bull : " Our temples,
by virtue of the divine sacrifice which is celebrated in them, are called houses of prayer;
they must therefore be held in the greatest
respect. Having received from God the
sure keeping of all the churches in the
Catholic world, it is our duty to banish
every profane and indecent act from these
churches. We have recently learned that
the bad habit of taking the herb commonly
called tobacco, by the mouth or nose, has
spread to such a degree in some dioceses
that persons of both sexes, even the priests
and clerks, both secular and regular, for-
getting that decorum which is due to their
rank, take tobacco everywhere, principally
in the churches of the town and diocese

of Seville ; nay, even—and we blush for
very shame—whilst celebrating the most
holy sacrifice of the mass.   They soil the
sacred linen with the disgusting humours
provoked by tobacco, they poison our
temples with a repulsive odour, to the
great scandal of their brethren who per-
severe in well-doing, nor do they seem to
dread their want of respect for all sacred
objects.

" Thus it is, that being wishful, and in
our anxiety, to remove so scandalous an
abuse from the temples of God, by virtue
of our Apostolic authority and by the
tenor of these presents, we interdict and
forbid all generally and each one in particular, persons of either sex, seculars, eccles-
iastics, every religious order, and all those
forming a portion of any religious institution whatsoever, to take tobacco in the
future in the porches or interiors of the
churches, whether by chewing, smoking or
inhaling it in the form of powder, in short
to use it in any shape or form whatsoever.
If any one contravene these provisions, let
him be excommunicated."

Several bishops, fully persuaded that
excommunication was insufficient to arrest
the practice, resolved to exact a heavy fine
from each parishioner who made use of
tobacco in church.   Elizabeth, Queen of

Spain, took a still more efficacious measure to suppress this unseemly indulgence, for she authorised the beadles to confiscate to their own use and profit the snuff-boxes of those who should make use of it during the solemnization of the mass.

----

### THE SNUFF-MULL IN THE SCOTCH KIRK.

AN English lady found herself in a parish church not far from Craithie, in a large pew occupied by farmers and their wives and one or two herdsmen—about a dozen in all. Just before the commencement of the sermon a large snuff-mull was handed round ; and upon the stranger declining to take a pinch, an old shepherd whispered significantly, " Tak' the snceshin', mem ; tak' the sneeshin'. Ye dinna ken oor minister ; ye'll need it afore he's dune."

----

### WHATELY AS A SNUFF-TAKER.

" THE logic class is assembled. The door by which the principal is to enter is exactly opposite to the foot

of the stair which descends from his own
apartment. It stands open, and presently
a kind of rushing sound is heard on the
staircase. The next instant, Whately
plunges headforemost into the room, saying
while yet in the doorway, 'Explain the nature
of the third operation of the mind, Mr.
Johnson.' But as none of the operations
of Mr. Johnson's mind are so rapid as those
of the energetic principal, the latter has had
time to fling himself into a chair, cross the
small of one leg over the knee of the
other, balance himself on the two hind
legs of the chair, and begin to show signs
of impatience, before Mr. Johnson has
sufficiently gathered his wits together.
While that process is being accomplished,
the principal soothes his impatience by
the administration of a huge pinch—or
handful, rather — of snuff to his nose,
copiously sprinkling his waistcoat with the
superfluity thereof. Then at last comes
from Mr. Johnson a meagre answer in
the words of the text-book, which is
followed by a luminous exposition of the
rationale of the whole of that part of the
subject, in giving which the lecturer
shoots far over the heads of the majority
of his hearers, but is highly appreciated
by the select few who are able to follow
him."

### THE FIRST BISHOP WHO SMOKED.

RICHARD FLETCHER (father of
John Fletcher the dramatist), a
courtly prelate whom Elizabeth, after pro-
moting him to the see of London, sus-
pended for marrying a second wife, was
the first Episcopal smoker in England.
Born in Kent, he rose to high favour at
Court (though the Queen on one occasion
found fault with him for cutting his beard
too short), until his unlucky marriage drew
upon him the severe sentence which
banished him to Chelsea. Here he
" smothered his cares," as Camden says,
" by immoderate use of tobacco ;" and
ere he could reinstate himself in the good
graces of a Queen " who did not so well
like of married bishops," he died suddenly, smoking his pipe in his easy-chair.

---

### PIGS AND SMOKERS.

" BROTHER G——," said one clergy-
man to another, "is it possible
you smoke tobacco? Pray, give up the
unseemly practice. It is alike unclerical
and uncleanly. Tobacco ! Why, my dear

brother, even a pig would not smoke so vile a weed !" Brother G—— delivered a mild out-pouring of tobacco-fumes, and then as mildly said, " I suppose, Brother C——, you don't smoke ?" " No, indeed !" exclaimed his friend, with virtuous horror. Another puff or two, and then Brother G——, who prefers the Socratic method of argument, rejoined, " Then, dear brother, which is more like the pig—you or I ? "

———

## JESUITS' SNUFF.

SCENTED snuffs were sometimes made to conceal poison. In 1712 the Duc de Noailles presented the Dauphiness of France with a box of Spanish snuff, a luxury in which she delighted. It was charged with poison, which she inhaled ; and five days after receiving the gift she died. complaining of sharp pain in the temples. This excited much attention, and great fear prevailed of "accepting a pinch " on the one hand and offering it on the other. It became a general belief that such poisoned snuff was used in Spain, and by Spanish emissaries, to clear away political opponents, and that the Jesuits also adopted it for the purpose of

B

secretly poisoning their enemies. Hence it was termed " Jesuits' Snuff," and a great dread of it was felt for a considerable time. Another instance of the fatal use of snuff is to be found in an anecdote of the Duc de Bourbon, grandson of the great Condé. He took Santeuil the poet to a great entertainment, compelled him to drink a large quantity of champagne, and ultimately poured his snuff-box, filled with Spanish snuff, into the poet's wine. This produced a violent fever, of which Santeuil died, amid excruciating agonies, within fourteen hours.

## KEMBLE PIPES.

A POOR Roman Catholic priest, named Kemble, was hanged in 1679, in his eightieth year, he having been implicated in the plot of Titus Oates. He marched to his fate, amidst a crowd of weeping friends, with the tranquillity of a primitive martyr, and smoking a pipe of tobacco. In memory of this, the people of Herefordshire to this day call the last pipe they take at a sitting a Kemble pipe.

## AN INGENIOUS SMOKER.

THE famous Bishop Burnet, like many authors of later days, was very partial to tobacco, and always smoked while he was writing. In order to combine the two operations with perfect comfort to himself, he would bore a hole through the broad brim of his large hat, and, putting the stem of his long pipe through it, puff and write, and write and puff, with learned gravity. This singular device, however, did not originate with the English divine, since Heine concludes some ponderous joking on those who have liked and those who have disliked tobacco (among the latter he himself being included), with the remark that the great Boxhornius also loved tobacco, and that "in smoking he wore a hat with a broad brim, in the fore-part of which he had a hole, through which the pipe was stuck, that it might not hinder his studies." This famous scholar and critic, who died at Leyden in 1653, was wont, with the modesty of genuine erudition, to say : "How many things there are that we do not know !" Whereupon some one has remarked that there was one thing certainly that Box-hornius did not know, and that was how to moderate himself in the use of tobacco, inasmuch as by smoking incessantly he shortened his life.

---

### ANECDOTE OF DEAN ALDRICH.

DR. ALDRICH, the Oxford Professor of Music, was an inveterate smoker, and in the university the following story, among others, passed current :

A young student of the college, once finding some difficulty in persuading a friend of his upon the point, laid him a wager that the Dean would be found smoking at ten o'clock in the morning. Away, therefore, at the appointed hour, went the student to the Deanery, where, being admitted to the Dean in his study, he related the occasion of his visit, to which the Dean replied, in perfect good humour : "You see you have lost your wager, for I'm not smoking, but filling my pipe."

In the *Pleasant Musical Companion,* printed in 1726, are two catches of Dr Aldrich's, the one, "Hark, the bonny Christ Church bells," the other, "A Smoking catch, to be sung by four men smoking their pipes, not more difficult to

sing than diverting to hear." The catch
above mentioned was written and composed to be sung by the Dean, Mr. Samp-
son Estwick, then of Christ Church, and
afterwards of St. Paul's, and two other
smoking friends.

--------

### SMOKING TO THE GLORY OF GOD.

ONE Sunday evening Mr. Spurgeon,
   before beginning his sermon at the
Metropolitan Tabernacle, announced that
he should not preach long that night, because he wished his friend Mr. Pentecost,
who was on the platform, to say a few
words to the congregation. Mr. Spurgeon
then gave a very earnest address on the
words, " I cried with my whole heart;
hear me, O Lord; I will keep thy
statutes. I cried unto thee ; save me,
and I shall keep thy testimonies" (Ps.
cxix. 145-6). He spoke strongly and
plainly upon the necessity of giving up
sin, in order to success in prayer for
"quickening," and as an evidence of
sincerity. Mr. Spurgeon, in concluding
his discourse, said, " Now, then, perhaps
Brother Pentecost will give you the application of that sermon."

"Brother Pentecost" is an "open communion" Baptist minister, of the American city of Boston. He responded at once to Mr. Spurgeon's call, and, stepping to the front of the platform, made some appropriate comments on the latter portion of the text, speaking with much simplicity and force. Referring to one part of Mr. Spurgeon's sermon, he gave an interesting bit of personal experience. He said that some years ago he had had the cry awakened in his heart, "Quicken thou me." He desired to be more completely delivered from sin, and he prayed that God would show him anything which prevented his more complete devotion to him. He was willing, he thought, to give up anything or everything, if only he might realise the desire of his heart. "Well," said he, amid the profound silence and attention of the immense congregation, "what do you think it was that the Lord required of me? He did not touch me in my church, my family, my property, or my passions. But one thing I liked exceedingly — the best cigar that could be bought." He then said that the thought came into his mind, could he relinquish this indulgence, if its relinquishment would advance his piety? He tried to dismiss the idea as a mere foolish fancy, but it

came again and again to him, and he was
satisfied that it was the still small voice
which was speaking. "He remembered
having given up smoking by the wish of
his ministerial brethren, when he was
twenty-one, for four years. But then he
had resumed the habit, for he declared
that during those four years he never saw
or smelt a cigar which he did not want to
smoke. Now, however, he felt it to be
his duty to give it up again, and so
unequal did he feel to the self-denial, that
he "took his cigar-box before the Lord,"
and cried to him for help. This help
he intimated had been given, and the
habit was renounced.

Mr. Spurgeon, whose smoking propensities are pretty well known, instantly rose
at the conclusion of Mr. Pentecost's
address, and, with a somewhat playful
smile, said : "Well, dear friends, you
know that some men can do to the glory
of God what in other men would be sin.
And notwithstanding what Brother Pentecost has said, I intend to smoke a good
cigar to the glory of God before I go to
bed to-night. If anybody can show me
in the Bible the command, 'Thou shalt
not smoke,' I am ready to keep it ; but I
haven't found it yet. I find ten command-
ments. and it's as much as I can do to

keep them ; and I've no desire to make
them into eleven or twelve. The fact is
that I have been speaking to you about
real sins, not about mere quibbles and
scruples. At the same time I know that
what a man believes to be a sin becomes
a sin to him, and he must give it up.
' Whatsoever is not of faith is sin,' and
that is the real point of what my brother
Pentecost has been saying. Why, a man
may think it is a sin to have his boots
blacked. Well, then, let him give it up,
and have them whitewashed. I wish to
say that I'm not ashamed of anything
whatever that I do, and I don't feel that
smoking makes me ashamed, and therefore I mean to smoke to the glory of
God."

Great was the scandal produced by this
manly utterance of the great preacher ; but
he stuck to it, and wrote to the *Daily
Telegraph :* " As I would not knowingly
live even in the smallest violation of the
law of God—and sin is the transgression
of the law—I will not own to sin when I
am not conscious of it. There is growing
up in society a Pharisaic system which
adds to the commands of God the pre-
cepts of men ; to that system I will not
yield for an hour. The preservation of
my liberty may bring upon me the up-

braiding of many of the good, and the
sneers of the self-righteous; but I shall
endure both with serenity, so long as I feel
clear in my conscience before God.   The
expression, 'smoking to the glory of God,'
standing alone, has an ill sound, and I do
not justify it; but in the sense in which I
employed it, I shall stand to it.   No
Christian should do anything in which he
cannot glorify God; and this may be done,
according to Scripture, in eating, and
drinking, and the common actions of life.
When I have found intense pain relieved,
a weary brain soothed, and calm, refresh-
ing sleep obtained by a cigar, I have felt
grateful to God, and have blessed his
name; this is what I meant, and by no
means did I use sacred words triflingly.
If through smoking I had wasted an hour
of my time, if I had stinted my gifts to the
poor, if I had rendered my mind less
vigorous, I trust I should see my fault and
turn from it; but he who charges me with
these things shall have no answer but my
forgiveness.   I am told that my open
avowal will lessen my influence; and my
reply is that if I have gained any influence
through being thought different from what
I am, I have no wish to retain it.   I will
do nothing upon the sly, and nothing
about which I have a doubt.   I am most

sorry that prominence has been given to what seems to me so small a matter, and the last thing in my thoughts would have been the mention of it from the pulpit; but I was placed in such a position that I must either by my silence plead guilty to living in sin, or else bring down upon my unfortunate self the fierce rebukes of the anti-tobacco advocates by speaking out honestly. I chose the latter; and although I am now the target for these worthy brethren, I would sooner endure their severest censures than sneakingly do what I could not justify, and earn immunity from their criticisms by tamely submitting to be charged with sin in an action which my conscience allows."

---

## PROFESSOR HUXLEY ON SMOKING.

AT a debate upon "Smoking," among the members of the British Association, many speakers denounced and others advocated the practice. Professor Huxley said, " For forty years of my life, tobacco has been a deadly poison to me. (*Loud cheers from the anti-tobacconists.*)  In my youth, as a medical student, I tried to smoke.   In vain !  at every fresh attempt my insidious foe stretched me prostrate on the floor.   (*Repeated cheers.*)   I entered the navy ; again I tried to smoke, and again met with a defeat.   I hated tobacco.   I could almost have lent my support to any institution that had for its object the putting of tobacco-smokers to death.   (*Vociferous applause.*)   A few years ago I was in Brittany with some friends.   We went to an inn.   They began to smoke.   They looked very happy, and outside it was very wet and dismal.   I thought I would try a cigar.   (*Murmurs.*)   I did so.   (*Great expectations.*)   I smoked that cigar—it was delicious !   (*Groans.*)   From that moment I was a changed man ; and I now feel that smoking in moderation is a comfortable and laudable practice, and is productive of good.   (*Dismay and confusion of the anti-tobacconists.   Roars of laughter from the smokers.*)   There is no more harm in a pipe than there is in a cup of tea.   You may poison yourself by drinking too much green tea, and kill yourself by eating too many beef-steaks.   For my own part, I consider that tobacco, in moderation, is a sweetener and equaliser of the temper."   (*Total rout of the anti-tobacconists, and complete triumph of the smokers.*)

## BLÜCHER'S PIPE-MASTER.

BLÜCHER'S 'pipe-master,' at the time of the Liberation War, was Christian Hennemann, a Mecklenburger from Rostock, like Blücher himself, and most devotedly attached to the Field-marshal. He knew all the characteristic peculiarities of the old hero; and no one could so skilfully adapt himself to them. His duties as pipe-master Hennemann discharged with a fidelity approaching fanatical zeal. The contents of the pipe-chest he thoroughly knew, for he often counted the pipes. Before every fight, Prince Blucher usually ordered a long pipe to be filled. After smoking for a short time, he gave back the lighted pipe to Hennemann, placed himself in the saddle, drew his sabre, and with the vigorous cry, " Forward, my lads !" threw himself fiercely on the foe. On the ever memorable day of the Battle of Waterloo, Hennemann had just handed a pipe to his master, when a cannon-ball struck the ground near, so that earth and sand covered Blücher and his grey horse. The horse made a spring to one side, and the new pipe was broken before the old hero had taken a single puff.

"Fill another pipe for me," said Blücher, "keep it lighted, and wait for me here a moment, till I drive away the French rascals. Forward, lads !" Thereupon there was a rush forwards ; but the chase lasted not merely a moment, but a whole hot day. At the Belle Alliance Inn, which was demolished by shot, the victorious generals, Blücher and Wellington, met and congratulated each other on the grand and nobly achieved work, each praising the bravery of the other's troops. "Your fellows slash in like the very devil himself;" cried Wellington. Blücher replied, "Yes, you see that is their business. But brave as they are, I know not whether one of them would stand as firmly and calmly in the midst of the shower of bullets as your English." Wellington then asked Blücher about his previous position, which had enabled him to execute an attack so fatal to the enemy. Blücher, who could strike tremendous blows, but was by no means a finished orator, and could not paint his deeds in words, conducted Wellington to the place itself. They found it deserted ; but on the very spot where Blücher had that morning halted, and from which he had galloped away, stood a man with his head bound up and his arm wrapped in a handkerchief. He was smoking a long and dazzlingly white clay pipe. " Good God ! " exclaimed Blucher, "that is my servant, Christian Hennemann. What a strange look you have, man ! What are you doing here ? " " Have you come at last ? " answered Christian, in a grumbling tone ; " here I have stood the whole day waiting for you. One pipe after another has been shot away from my mouth by the accursed French. Once even a blue bean (bullet) made sad work with my head, and my fist has got a deuce of a smashing. That is the last whole pipe, and it is a good thing that the firing has ceased ; otherwise the French would have knocked this pipe to pieces, and you must have stood there with a dry mouth."

We cannot, we should add, vouch for the absolute historical accuracy of this very Munchhausen-like anecdote.

----

## SHAKESPEARE AND TOBACCO.

IT is a curious fact that no allusion to " divine Tobacco," as Spenser calls it, is to be found in the works of Shakespeare, though Ben Jonson and his contemporaries indulge in jests at the expense of the lately-imported weed, which was smoked

under the very noses of the players by the
gilded youth of the period, who were wont
to take up their positions upon the stage,
where stools were placed for them, and
smoke incessantly during the whole per-
formance.

Shakespeare being the favourite play-
wright of James I., whose hatred of
smoking is well-known, it is not surprising
that he failed to notice it favourably in
the days of that monarch ; but that the
companion of Raleigh and Bacon at the
" Mermaid " should have nothing to say
upon the subject is an enigma which some
future Shakespearean scholar may perhaps
unravel.

---

### BEN JONSON ON TOBACCO.

" SIR, believe me, upon my relation, for
what I tell you the world shall not
reprove.    I have been in the Indies, where
this herb grows, where neither myself, nor
a dozen gentlemen more of my knowledge, have received the taste of any
other nutriment in the world for the space
of one-and-twenty weeks but the fume
of this simple only : therefore it cannot
be but 'tis most divine.    I do hold it,

and will affirm it before any prince in Europe, to be *the most sovereign and precious weed that ever the earth tendered to the use of man."—Captain Bobadil, in " Every Man in his Humour "* (1598).

———

## LORD BYRON ON TOBACCO.

BORNE from a short frail pipe which yet had blown
Its gentle odours over either zone,
And, puff'd where'er winds rise or waters roll,
Had wafted smoke from Portsmouth to the Pole,
Opposed its vapour as the lightning flash'd,
And reek'd, midst mountain-billows unabash'd,
To Æolus a constant sacrifice,
Thro' every change of all the varying skies.
And what was he who bore it ?   I may err,
But deem him sailor or philosopher.
SUBLIME TOBACCO ! which from East to West
Cheers the tar's labour or the Turkman's rest ;
Which on the Moslem's ottoman divides

His hours, and rivals opium and his
    brides ;
Magnificent in Stamboul, but less grand,
Though not less loved, in Wapping or the
    Strand ;
Divine in hookahs, glorious in a pipe,
When tipp'd with amber, mellow, rich,
    and ripe ;
Like other charmers, wooing the caress,
More dazzlingly when daring in full dress ;
Yet thy true lovers more admire by far
Thy naked beauties—give me a cigar !
       " *The Island* " (*Canto II., sect. xix.*).

———

### DÉCAMPS AND HORACE VERNET.

A CRITIC once discovered that the
great difference between two celebrated French painters, Décamps and
Horace Vernet, was mainly the effect of
their habits as users of tobacco. The
French Murillo, the Oriental colourist, the
sublime Décamps, smoked a pipe. Vernet
toyed with the cigarette.

———

### MILTON'S PIPE.

MILTON was a smoker. When composing " Paradise Lost," he portioned out each day in the following manner :—As soon as he rose, a chapter of the Bible was read out to him (he was *then* blind). He afterwards studied till twelve, taking an hour's exercise before he dined. After dinner, he devoted himself to music, playing on the organ, and he then resumed his studies till six o'clock. Visitors were received from six till eight, at which hour he supped, and having had his pipe of tobacco and glass of water, he retired for the night.

---

### ANECDOTE OF SIR ISAAC NEWTON.

THIS great natural philosopher was also a prince among smokers, and, as if to expose the fallacy of one of the many objections to tobacco—viz., that it injures the teeth—he lived to a good old age, and never lost but a single tooth. It is recorded of him that on one occasion, in a fit of mental abstraction, he used

the finger of the lady he was courting as
a tobacco-stopper, as he sat and smoked
in silence beside her!

---

## EMERSON AND CARLYLE.

THE friendship formed by these two
men at Craigenputtock lasted during their lives. There is an unpublished
legend to the effect that on the one evening passed at Craigenputtock by Emerson,
in 1833, Carlyle gave him a pipe, and,
taking one himself, the two sat silent till
midnight, and then parted, shaking hands,
with congratulations on the profitable and
pleasant evening they had enjoyed.

---

## PALEY AND HIS PIPE.

PALEY had one of the most orderly
minds ever given to man. A vein
of shrewd and humorous sarcasm, together
with an under-current of quiet selfishness,
made him a very pleasant companion.
"I cannot afford to keep a conscience
any more than a carriage," he said. "Our
delight was," writes an old Johnian who

knew him well, " to get old Paley on a cold winter's night to put up his legs, stir the fire, and fill a long Dutch pipe. He would talk away, sir, like a being of a higher sphere. He formally declined any punch, but nevertheless drank it up as fast as we replenished his glass. He would smoke any given quantity of tobacco, and drink any given quantity of punch."

----

### JULES SANDEAU ON THE CIGAR.

THE cigar is one of the greatest triumphs of the old world over the new. It would be curious to trace the origin of the cigar, to watch its gradual development, and to observe its rapid growth and wide distribution. We might study, too, all the transformations it has undergone in passing from the homely lips of the commonalty to the rose-coloured lips of our dandies. Indeed, its history would not be wholly devoid of interest, for no epoch, perhaps, can show an example of fortune so rapid as that of the cigar. The cigar is ubiquitous ; it is the indispensable complement of all idle and elegant life ; the man who does not smoke cannot be regarded as perfect. The cigar of to-day has taken the place of the little romances, coffee and verses of the seventeenth century. I am not talking of the primitive cigar, whose poisonous odour and acrid and repulsive flavour reached one's martyred lips through the tube of a straw. Civilisation has truly altered such early simplicity. Spain, Turkey and Havana have yielded up to us the most precious treasures of their smoke-enwrapt dreamland! and our lips can now filter the perfumed vapour of odoriferous leaves which have crossed the sea at our summons. Do not ask me to describe the charms of the reverie, or the contemplative ecstasy into which the smoke of our cigar plunges us. Words are powerless to express or define these " states ; " they are vague and mysterious, as unseizable as the sweetly-scented clouds which are emitted from your " mexico " or your "panatella." Only let me tell you that if you have never found yourself extended upon a divan with soft and downy cushions, on some winter's evening, before a clear and sparkling fire, enveloping the globe of your lamp or the white light of your wax-candle, with the smoke of a well-seasoned cigar, letting your thoughts ascend as uncertain and vaporous as the smoke float-

ing around you, let me tell you, I repeat,
that if you have never yet enjoyed this
situation, you still have to be initiated into
one of the sweetest of our terrestrial joys.
Casanova, that immodest Venetian who
wrote his own Memoirs, so that no one
should be able to discover any eccentricity
he had not committed, pretends that the
smoker's sole pleasure consists in seeing
the smoke escape from his lips. I think,
O Venetian! that you have touched a false
note here. The smoke of the cigar produces the same effect as opium, in that it
leads to a state of febrile exaltation, a
perennial source of new pleasures. The
cigar deadens sorrow, distracts our enforced inactivity, renders idleness sweet
and easy to us, and peoples our solitude
with a thousand gracious images. Solitude
without friend or cigar is indeed insupport-
able to those who suffer. For the rest, I am
obliged to admit that I know of no more
dangerous or profoundly immoral importa-
tion than the fashionable weed. It will be the
ruin of many a young man of good family ;
and the immorality of gaming houses and
houses of evil repute pales before that of the
cigar. It is through the fragrant weed that
we drift into indolence and become dreamy,
contemplative, useless creatures. These
delicately rolled leaves will work us more

harm than German literature, the loves of Werther, the fantastical dreams of René, or the fanciful recitals of Hoffmann.

Perhaps this seems somewhat paradoxical to you. Oh, well, smoke; reflect upon it afterwards if you can, and you shall then tell me whether a cigar does not offer as many dangers to a feeble spirit given to dreaming, as the poetic egoism of Obermann.

The cigar which has insinuated itself into fashionable spheres has gained special sway over the artistic world, and has indeed converted it into an "annexe" of the Café Hollandais. The cigar constitutes the livery, the badge, the ensign, of the man of letters, and the wielder of the brush. Have you ever been present at the morning receptions of some contemporary celebrity? The fashionable lions of the day get up in a cloud of smoke. Our great men each morning receive a circle of admirers, who come to amuse the idol of the day and smoke in his face. But in so doing the admiring circle expends less wit than it consumes cigars ; and more smoke than glory is to be obtained from these *réunions.*

———

THE "PICKWICK" OF FLEET STREET.
THE *OBSEQUIO* OF HAVANA.

AT Havana, when a distinguished
stranger visits the tobacco factory
of Señor Cabana or Partagas, the custom
is to offer him an " obsequio," by fashion-
ing a new brand of cigars in his honour.
To this we owe the excellent cigars known
as the "Serrano," and the "Henry
Clay;" and had the great leaders of
the Conservative and the Liberal parties
visited Havana, Señores Anselmo del
Valle and Partagas would soon have
consigned "Gladstones" or "Juventus
Mundis," "Disraelis" or "Lothairs" to
the European market. The London
tobacco manufacturers elected to pay
Charles Dickens the Cuban compliment.
A neat little cigar, costing only a penny,
was devised, and christened the "Pickwick;" which still retains its popularity.
Such an ingenious stretch of courtesy has
not been equalled, save by the patriotic
coach-builder who constructed a four-
wheeled cab of a novel shape, and dubbed
it a "Brougham."

### THE SOCIAL PIPE.

HONEST men, with pipes or cigars in their mouths, have great physical advantages in conversation. You may stop talking if you like, but the breaks of silence never seem disagreeable, being filled up by the puffing of the smoke ; hence there is no awkwardness in resuming the conversation, no straining for effect—sentiments are delivered in a grave, easy manner. The cigar harmonises the society, and soothes at once the speaker and the subject whereon he converses. I have no doubt that it is from the habit of smoking that Turks and American-Indians are such monstrous well-bred men. The pipe draws wisdom from the lips of the philosopher, and shuts up the mouth of the foolish ; it generates a style of conversation, contemplative, thoughtful, benevolent, and unaffected ; in fact, dear Bob,—I must out with it—I am an old smoker. At home, I have done it up the chimney rather than not do it (the which, I own, is a crime).

I vow and believe that the cigar has been one of the greatest creature-comforts of my life—a kind companion, a gentle stimulant, an amiable anodyne, a cementer

C

of friendship.   May I die if I abuse that
kindly weed which has given me so much
pleasure.—*Thackeray.*

———

### TRIUMPH OF TOBACCO OVER SACK AND ALE.

WE reproduce seven characteristic
verses from the " Triumph of
Tobacco over Sack and Ale" (a ballad),
from a collection entitled " Wits' Recrea-
tions," originally published in 1640 :—

Tobacco engages
Both sexes, all ages,
    The poor as well as the wealthy ;
From the court to the cottage,
From childhood to dotage,
    Both those that are sick and the healthy.

It plainly appears
That in a few years
    Tobacco more custom hath gain'd
Than sack or than ale,
Though they double the tale
    Of the times wherein they have reign'd.

And worthily too,
For what they undo,
　　Tobacco doth help to regain,
On fairer conditions
Than many physicians,
　　Puts an end to much grief and pain.


It helpeth digestion,
Of that there's no question;
　　The gout and the toothache it eases;
Be it early or late,
'Tis ne'er out of date,
　　He may safely take it that pleases.


Tobacco prevents
Infections by scents,
　　That hurt the brain and are heavy,
An antidote is
Before you're amiss,
　　As well as an after remedy.


The cold it doth heat,
Cools them that do sweat,
　　And them that are fat maketh lean,
The hungry doth feed,
And if there be need,
　　Spent spirits restoreth again.


The Poets of old
Many Fables have told,
　　Of the gods and their symposia,

But Tobacco alone,
Had they known it, had gone
    For their *Nectar* and *Ambrosia*.

----

### THE SMOKING PHILOSOPHER.

H IS whole amusement was his pipe ;
    and, as there is a certain inde-
finable link between smoking and philo-
sophy, my father, by dint of smoking, had
become a perfect philosopher. It is no
less strange than true that we can
puff away our cares with tobacco, when,
without it, they remain an oppressive
burthen to existence. There is no composing draught like the draught through
the tube of a pipe. The savage warriors
of North America enjoyed the bless-
ing before we did ; and to the pipe is to
be ascribed the wisdom of their councils,
and the laconic delivery of their sentiments.
It would be well introduced into our own
legislative assembly. Ladies, indeed, would
no longer peep down through the ven-
tilator ; but we should have more sense
and fewer words. It is also to tobacco
that is to be ascribed the stoical firmness
of those American warriors who, satisfied
with the pipe in their mouths, submitted

with perfect indifference to the torture of
their enemies. From the well-known virtues
of this weed arose that peculiar expression,
when you irritate another, that you " put
his pipe out."—*Marryat's "Jacob Faithful."*

---

SAM SLICK ON THE VIRTUES OF A PIPE.

" THE fact is, squire, the moment a
man takes to a pipe he becomes a
philosopher. It's the poor man's friend ; it
calms the mind, soothes the temper, and
makes a man patient under difficulties. It
has made more good men, good husbands,
kind masters, indulgent fathers, than any
other blessed thing on this universal earth."
—*" Sam Slick, the Clockmaker."*

---

SMOKING IN 1610.

FROM the following passage in Ben
Jonson's play, " The Alchemist,"
first acted in 1610, we gather some curious
particulars respecting the business of a
tobacconist of that period. It occurs in
the first Act, where Abel Drugger is introduced to Subtle :

" This is my friend Abel, an honest fellow ;
He lets me have good tobacco, and he does not
Sophisticate it with sack-lees or oil,

Nor washes it in muscadel and grains,
Nor buries it in gravel, underground,
Wrapt up in greasy leather,  . . . . .
But keeps it in fine lily pots that, open'd,
Smell like conserve of roses, or French beans.
He has his maple block, his silver tongs,
Winchester pipes, and fire of juniper :
A neat, spruce, honest fellow.  .  .  "

The Virginian tobacco was usually imported in the leaf, and had to be rubbed small for smoking. The Spanish tobacco was manufactured into balls about the size of a man's head, and was also imported in the form of what the French term *carottes*, which were known in England by an obscene name, hardly yet obsolete among sailors. Not fifty years ago a story was current in the West Indies of a facetious reply given by a sailor to his captain's wife, who, happening to see him employed about some tobacco, asked him what he was going to make of it : "*Penem volo fabricari, domina, sed vereor ne ex illo coleos faciam.*" This carotte and ball tobacco was cut as required into small pieces on a maple-block with a knife, and the pipe—shorter and straighter in the stem and more upright in the bowl than those of our own day—being filled, was lighted by embers of juniper wood, taken from a kind of chafing dish by silver tongs.

## BULWER-LYTTON ON TOBACCO-SMOKING.

HE who doth not smoke hath either known no great griefs, or refuseth himself the softest consolation, next to that which comes from heaven. " What softer than woman ? " whispers the young reader. Young reader, woman teases as well as consoles. Woman makes half the sorrows which she boasts the privilege to soothe. Woman consoles us, it is true, while we are young and handsome ; when we are old and ugly, woman snubs and scolds us. On the whole, then, woman in this scale, the weed in that, Jupiter ! hang out thy balance, and weigh them both ; and if thou give the preference to woman, all I can say is, the next time Juno ruffles thee, O Jupiter ! try the weed.—"*What will he do with it ?*"

## PROFESSOR SEDGWICK.

SIR J. W. KAYE gives the following account of a visit he paid to Dr. Whewell and Professor Sedgwick at Cambridge five-and-twenty years ago. He

dined with Whewell and went to take tea
with Sedgwick.

"I joined him (he was quite alone) in the
dress in which I had dined. He also was
in evening costume. We drank some tea,
but conversation flagged. I had heard
much of his fund of anecdote, of his vivid
memory and choice reminiscences, and I
was disappointed. But presently it
occurred to me that I had been told he was
a great smoker, an impression which the
pervading odour of his room amply confirmed. So I said to him, 'I think, Professor, that you like your pipe in the evening?' 'Yes,' he answered, 'do you
smoke?' I replied, 'I enjoy a smoke.'
Upon which he got up, brought me a box
of cigars, helped me to take off my dress-
coat, gave me a light smoking robe in its
place, rang the bell, sent away the tea, and
called for brandy-and-water. Then the
talk began in earnest. Each in an easy-
chair, we sat for hours—hours that I shall
not easily forget. I was well content to
be silent, except so far as I could lead the
Professor on, by a question or a sugges-
tion, to some stories of his early days."

OPINION OF ST. PIERRE ON THE EFFECT OF
TOBACCO.

THE author of "Paul and Virginia"
remarks, "It is true that tobacco
in some measure augments our power of
judgment by exciting the nerves of the
brain. This plant is, however, a veritable
poison, and in the long run affects the
sense of smell and sometimes the nerves
of the eye. But man is always ready to
impair his physical constitution provided
he can strengthen his "intellectual senti-
ment" thereby.

———

ODE TO TOBACCO.

THOU who, when fears attack,
       Bidst them avaunt, and black
Care, at the horseman's back
       Perching, unseatest ;
Sweet when the morn is grey;
Sweet, when they've clear'd away
Lunch ; and at close of day
       Possibly sweetest:

I have a liking old
For thee, though manifold
Stories, I know, are told,
  Not to thy credit;
How one (or two at most)
Drops make a cat a ghost—
Useless, except to roast—
  Doctors have said it :

How they who use fusees
All grow by slow degrees
Brainless as chimpanzees,
  Meagre as lizards,
Go mad, and beat their wives ;
Plunge (after shocking lives)
Razors and carving knives
  Into their gizzards :

Confound such knavish tricks !
Yet know I five or six
Smokers who freely mix
  Still with their neighbours;
Jones (who, I'm glad to say,
Ask'd leave of Mrs. J—)
Daily absorbs a clay
  After his labours :

Cats may have had their goose
Cooked by tobacco-juice ;
Still why deny its use
  Thoughtfully taken ?

We're not as tabbies are :
Smith, take a fresh cigar !
Jones, the tobacco-jar !
    Here's to thee, Bacon!
        *C. S. Calverley.*

––––––

## MEAT AND DRINK.

THEY had gone ten miles or more ;
the day began to draw in, and the
vestern wind to sweep more cold and cheer-
less every moment, when Amyas, knowing
that there was not an inn for many a mile
ahead, took a pull at a certain bottle
which Lady Grenvile had put into his
holster, and then offered Yeo a pull also.
He declined ; he had meat and drink too
about him, Heaven be praised ! "Meat
and drink ? fall to then, man, and don't
stand on manners." Whereon Yeo, seeing an old decayed willow by a brook,
went to it and took therefrom some touch-
wood, to which he set a light with his knife
and a stone, while Amyas watched, a little
puzzled and startled, as Yeo's fiery reputa-
tion came into his mind. Was he really
a Salamander-Sprite, and going to warm
his inside by a meal of burning tinder ?

But now Yeo, in his solemn methodical
way, pulled out of his bosom a brown leaf,
and began rolling a piece of it up neatly
to the size of his little finger; and then,
putting the one end into his mouth and
the other on the tinder, sucked at it till it
was a-light, and drinking down the smoke,
began puffing it out again at his nostrils,
with a grunt of deepest satisfaction, and
resumed his dog-trot by Amyas' side, as
if he had been a walking chimney.  On
which Amyas burst into a loud laugh, and
cried, "Why, no wonder they said you
breathed fire !  Is not that the Indian.'
tobacco ? "

"Yea, verily, Heaven be praised ! bu
did you never see it before ? "

"Never, though we heard talk of it
along the coast ; but we took it for one
more Spanish lie.   Humph—well, live and
learn ! "

"Ah ! sir, no lie, but a blessed truth, as
I can tell, who have ere now gone in the
strength of this weed three days and nights
without eating ; and therefore, sir, the
Indians always carry it with them on their
war-parties ; and no wonder, for when all
things were made, none was made better
than this, to be a lone man's companion,
a bachelor's friend, a hungry man's food, a
sad man's cordial, a wakeful man's sleep, and

a chilly man's fire, sir ; while for stanching
of wounds, purging of rheum, and settling
of the stomach, there's no herb like unto it
under the canopy of heaven."—*Charles
Kingsley, " Westward Ho !"* (1855, *vol. i.,
pp.* 271-272).

---

### THE MEERSCHAUM.

CERTAIN things are good for nothing
until they have been kept a long
while ; and some are good for nothing
until they have been long kept and *used.*
Of the first, wine is the illustrious and
immortal example. Of those which must
be kept and used, I will name three—
meerschaum pipes, violins, and poems.
The meerschaum is but a poor affair until
it has burned a thousand offerings to the
cloud-compelling deities. It comes to us
without complexion or flavour, born of the
sea-foam, like Aphrodite, but colourless as
*pallida Mors* herself. The fire is lighted
in its central shrine, and gradually the
juices which the broad leaves of the great
vegetable had sucked up from an acre and
curdled into a drachm, are diffused through
its thirsting pores.

First, a discoloration, then a stain, and
at last a rich, glowing umber tint spreading

over the whole surface. Nature, true to
her old brown autumnal hue, you see—as
true in the fire of the meerschaum as in
the sunshine of October! And then the
cumulative wealth of its fragrant reminiscences! He who inhales its vapours takes a
thousand whiffs in a single breath ; and
one cannot touch it without awakening
the old joys that hang around it, as the
smell of flowers clings to the dresses of the
daughters of the house of Farina !

Don't think I use a meerschaum myself,
for I *do not*, though I have owned a
calumet since my childhood, which from
a naked Pict (of the Mohawk species) my
grandsire won, together with a tomahawk
and beaded knife-sheath ; paying for the
lot with a bullet-mark on his right cheek.
On the maternal side, I inherit the loveliest
silver-mounted tobacco-stopper you ever
saw. It is a little box-wood Triton, carved
with charming liveliness and truth ; I have
often compared it to a figure in Raphael's
"Triumph of Galatea." It came to me
in an ancient shagreen case; how old it is
I do not know, but it must have been
made since Sir Walter Raleigh's time. If
you are curious, you shall see it any day.
Neither will I pretend that I am so unused
to the more perishable smoking contrivance,
that a few whiffs would make me feel as if

I lay in a ground-swell on the Bay of
Biscay. I am not unacquainted with that
fusiform, spiral-wound bundle of chopped
stems and miscellaneous incombustibles—
the *cigar*, so called, of the shops, which to
" draw " asks the suction - power of a
nursling infant Hercules, and to relish,
the leathery palate of an old Silenus. I
do not advise you, young man, even if my
illustration strike your fancy, to consecrate
the flower of your life to painting the bowl
of a pipe ; for, let me assure you, the stain
of a reverie-breeding narcotic may strike
deeper than you think for. I have seen
the green leaf of early promise grow
brown before its time under such nicotian
regimen, and thought the umbered meerschaum was dearly bought at the cost
of a brain enfeebled and a will enslaved.
—*Holmes's " Autocrat of the Breakfast
Table"* (*Boston*, 1858, *pp.* 114-116).

---

### CHARLES KINGSLEY AT EVERSLEY.

KINGSLEY would work himself into
a sort of white heat over the book
he was writing, till, too excited to write
more, he would calm himself down with a
pipe. He was a great smoker, and tobacco

was to him a needful sedative.   He always
used a long and clean "churchwarden,"
and these pipes used to be bought a
barrelful at a time.   They lurked in all
sorts of unexpected places.   A pipe would
suddenly be extracted from a bush in the
garden, all ready filled and lighted, as if
by magic, or one has even been drawn
from a whin-bush on the heath, some half
mile from the house.   But none was ever
smoked that was in any degree foul ; and
when there was a vast accumulation of old
pipes, enough to fill the barrel, they
were sent back again to the kiln to be re-
baked, and returned fresh and new.   This
gave him a striking simile, which in
"Alton Locke" he puts into the mouth
of James Crossthwaite :—

"Katie here believes in purgatory,
where souls are burnt clean again, like
'bacca pipe."

ROBERT BURNS'S SNUFF-BOX.

ROBERT BURNS was never happier
than when he could "pass a winter
evening under some venerable roof and

smoke a pipe of tobacco or drink water gruel." He also took it in snuff. Mr. Bacon, who kept a celebrated posting-house north of Dumfries, was his almost inseparable associate. Many a merry night did they spend together over their cups of foaming ale or bowls of whiskey-toddy, and on some of those occasions Burns composed several of his best convivial songs. The bard and the innkeeper became so attached to each other that, as a token of regard, Burns gave Bacon his snuff-box, which for many years had been his pocket companion. The knowledge of this gift was confined to a few of their jovial brethren. But after Bacon's death, in 1825, when his household furniture was sold by public auction, this snuff-box was offered amongst other trifles, and some one in the crowd at once bid a shilling for it. There was a general exclamation that it was not worth twopence, and the auctioneer seemed about to knock it down. He first looked, however, at the lid, and then read in a tremendous voice the following inscription upon it :—
" Robert Burns, officer of the Excise." Scarcely had he uttered the words, says one who was present at the sale, before shilling after shilling was rapidly and confusedly offered for this relic of Scotland's

great bard, the greatest anxiety prevailing ;
while the biddings rose higher and higher,
till the trifle was finally knocked down for
five pounds. The box was made of the
tip of a horn, neatly turned round at the
point; its lid is plainly mounted with
silver, on which the inscription is en-
graved.

---

ROBINSON CRUSOE'S TOBACCO.

*(THE JOURNAL)*

*June* 28, 1660.

NOW, as the apprehension of the return of my distemper terrified me
very much, it occurred to my thought
that the Brazilians take no physic but
their tobacco for almost all distempers ;
and I had a piece of a roll of tobacco in
one of the chests, which was quite cured,
and some also that was green and not
quite cured.

I went, directed by Heaven, no doubt ;
for in this chest I found a cure both for
soul and body. I opened the chest,
and found what I looked for, viz., the
tobacco; and as the few books I had
saved lay there too, I took out one of the

Bibles which I mentioned before, and which, to this time, I had not found leisure, or so much as inclination to look into ; I say, I took it out, and brought both that and the tobacco with me to the table.

What use to make of the tobacco, I knew not, as to my distemper, or whether it was good for it or no; but I tried several experiments with it, as if I was resolved it should hit one way or other. I first took a piece of a leaf, and chewed it in my mouth, which, indeed, at first almost stupified my brain, the tobacco being green and strong, and I had not been much used to it ; then I took some and steeped it an hour or two in some rum, and resolved to take a dose of it when I lay down ; and lastly, I burnt some upon a pan of coals, and held my nose close over the smoke of it as long as I could bear it, as well for the heat as the virtue of it, and I held out almost to suffocation.

In the interval of this operation, I took up the Bible and began to read ; but my head was too much disturbed with the tobacco to bear reading, at least at that time ; only, having opened the book casually, the first words that occurred to me were these : "Call on me in the day of trouble, and I will deliver ; and thou shalt glorify me."

The words were very apt to my case,
and made some impression upon my
thoughts at the time of reading them,
though not so much as they did afterwards ; for, as for being delivered, the
word had no sound, as I may say, to me.
The thing was so remote, so impossible, in
my apprehension of things, that I began
to say, as the children of Israel did when
they were promised flesh to eat, "Can
God spread a table in the wilderness?"
So I began to say : "Can God himself
deliver me from this place?" And as it
was not for many years that any hope
appeared, this prevailed very often upon
my thoughts. But, however, the words
made a great impression upon me, and
I mused upon them very often. It grew
now late, and the tobacco had, as I said,
dozed my head so much that I inclined
to sleep, so I left my lamp burning in the
cave, lest I should want anything in the
night, and went to bed. But before I
lay down, I did what I had never done in
all my life,—I kneeled down and prayed
to God to fulfil the promise to me, that if
I called upon him in the day of trouble,
he would deliver me. After my broken
and imperfect prayer was over, I drunk
the rum in which I had steeped the tobacco,
which was so strong and rank of the

tobacco that, indeed, I could scarce get
it down. Immediately upon this I went to
bed, and I found presently it flew up into
my head violently; but I fell into a sound
sleep and waked no more till, by the sun,
it must necessarily be near three o'clock
in the afternoon the next day; nay, to this
hour, I am partly of the opinion that I
slept all the next day and night, and till
almost three the day after; for, otherwise,
I know not how I should lose a day out of
my reckoning in the days of the week, as
it appeared, some years after, I had done;
for if I had lost it by crossing and re-
crossing the Line, I should have lost more
than a day; but in my account it was lost,
and I never knew which way.

Be that, however, one way or other,
when I awaked I found myself exceedingly
refreshed, and my spirits lively and cheer-
ful. When I got up I was stronger
than I was the day before, and my
stomach better, for I was hungry; and, in
short, I had no fit the next day, but continued much altered for the better.

### GUIZOT.

A LADY one evening calling on Guizot, the historian of France, found him absorbed in his pipe. In astonishment she exclaimed, "What! you smoke, and yet have arrived at so great an age?" "Ah, madame," replied the venerable statesman, "if I had not smoked, I should have been dead ten years ago."

### VICTOR HUGO.

VICTOR HUGO is another veteran of smokedom. Go when you will to pass an evening with him, you find him sacrificing at the shrine of Nicotia. You ring the bell; a tidy maid-servant answers the door; you are shown into a smartly-furnished apartment, rather parlour than drawing-room, where the poet, whom his guests address as "Master," is sitting by the fire, and you are, forthwith, cordially invited to join him in the "cultus" of the "plant divine of rarest virtue."

## BUCKLE AS A SMOKER.

HENRY THOMAS BUCKLE, the great historian of Civilization, was a smoker, and collected more curious historical facts about smoking and tobacco than any other writer. He found it so imperious a necessity to have his three cigars every day, that he said he could neither read, write, nor talk if compelled to forego, or even to miss the usual hour for indulging in them. As he could not smoke when walking, the effort being too great for his constitution, which was just as delicate and weak as his mind was sturdy and vigorous, he never visited any house where smoking indoors was objected to. Many a house that never tolerated a cigar before bore with one for his sake. A traveller, who once met him in the East, found him smoking Latakia out of a large red-clay pipe with an extremely long cherry stalk, and drinking coffee *à la turque*, with evident satisfaction.

———

## CARLYLE ON TOBACCO.

"TOBACCO smoke," says Carlyle, "is the one element in which, by our European manners, men can sit silent to-

gether without embarrassment, and where
no man is bound to speak one word
more than he has actually and veritably
got to say. Nay, rather every man is ad-
monished and enjoined by the laws of
honour, and even of personal ease, to
stop short of that point; at all events to
hold his peace and take to his pipe again,
the instant he *has* spoken his meaning, if
he chance to have any. The results of
which salutary practice, if introduced into
constitutional Parliaments, might evi-
dently be incalculable. The essence of
what little intellect and insight there is in
that room—we shall or can get nothing
more out of any Parliament—and sedative,
gently-soothing, gently-clarifying, tobacco-
smoke (if the room were well ventilated,
open atop, and the air kept good), with
the obligation to a *minimum* of speech,
surely gives human intellect and insight
the best chance they can have."

---

A POET'S PIPE.

*(From the French of Charles Baudelaire.)*

A POET'S pipe am I ;
    And my Abyssinian tint
Is an unmistakable hint
That he lays me not often by,

When his soul is with grief o'erworn,
I smoke like the cottage where
They are cooking the evening fare
For the labourer's return.

I enfold and cradle his soul
In the vapour moving and blue
That mounts from my fiery mouth ;
And there is power in my bowl
To charm his spirit and soothe,
And heal his weariness too.

*Richard Herne Shepherd.*

---

## A PIPE OF TOBACCO.

LITTLE tube of mighty power,
    Charmer of an idle hour,
Object of my warm desire,
Lip of wax, and eye of fire :
And thy snowy taper waist,
With my finger gently braced ;
And thy pretty swelling crest,
With my little stopper press'd,
And the sweetest bliss of blisses,
Breathing from thy balmy kisses.
Happy thrice, and thrice agen,
Happiest he of happy men ;
Who when agen the night returns,

When agen the taper burns ;
When agen the cricket's gay
(Little cricket, full of play),
Can afford his tube to feed
With the fragrant Indian weed ;
Pleasure for a nose divine,
Incense of the god of wine.
Happy thrice, and thrice agen,
Happiest he of happy men.

*Isaac Hawkins Browne* (1736).

### THE HEADSMAN'S SNUFF-BOX.

RUDOLF, professor of the headsman's
trade,
Alike was famous for his arm and blade.
One day a prisoner Justice had to kill
Knelt at the block to test the artist's skill,
Bare-arm'd, swart-visaged, gaunt, and
shaggy-brow'd,
Rudolf the headsman rose above the
crowd.
His falchion lighten'd with a sudden
gleam,
As the pike's armour flashes in the stream.
He sheathed his blade ; he turn'd as if to
go ;

The victim knelt, still waiting for the
    blow.
" Why strikest not ?    Perform thy mur-
    derous act."
The prisoner said.    (His voice was
    slightly crack'd.)
" Friend, I *have* struck," the artist straight
    replied ;
" Wait but one moment, and yourself
    decide."

He held his snuff-box—" Now, then, if
    you please ! "
The prisoner sniff'd, and with a crashing
    sneeze,
Off his head tumbled—bowl'd along the
    floor—
Bounced down the steps ;—the prisoner
    said no more.

                *Oliver Wendell Holmes.*

---

### SAYS THE PIPE TO THE SNUFF-BOX.

SAYS the Pipe to the Snuff-box, " I
    can't understand
What the ladies and gentlemen see in
    your face,
That you are in fashion all over the land,
And I am so much fallen into disgrace.

" Do but see what a pretty contemplative
    air
  I give to the company—pray do but note
      'em,—
You would think that the wise men of
    Greece were all there,
  Or, at least, would suppose them the
    wise men of Gotham.

" My breath is as sweet as the breath of
    blown roses,
  While you are a nuisance where'er you
    appear ;
There is nothing but snivelling and blow-
    ing of noses,
  Such a noise as turns any man's stomach
    to hear."

Then lifting his lid in a delicate way,
  And opening his mouth with a smile
    quite engaging,
The Box in reply was heard plainly to say,
  " What a silly dispute is this we are
    waging !

" If you have a little of merit to claim,
  You may thank the sweet-smelling Vir-
    ginian weed ;
And I, if I seem to deserve any blame,
  The before-mention'd drug in apology
    plead.

" Thus neither the praise nor the blame is
    our own,
  No room for a sneer, much less a
    cachinnus ;
We are vehicles not of tobacco alone,
  But of anything else they may choose to
    put in us."    *Cowper* (1782).

--------

### ANECDOTE OF CHARLES LAMB.

CHARLES LAMB was one day in
the height of his glory, puffing
away at the strongest and coarsest pre-
paration of the weed in company with
Dr. Parr, when the doctor who could
only smoke the finest sorts of tobacco
from his long clay pipe half filled with
salt, asked in astonishment how Charles
had acquired this " prodigious power?"
" I toiled after it," replied the humourist,
with his habitual stutter, " as some men
t-t-toil after virtue."

--------

### GIBBON AS A SNUFF-TAKER.

GIBBON, the historian of Rome, was
a confirmed snuff-taker, and in
one of his letters has left this account

of his mode of using it : " I drew my snuff-box, rapp'd it, took snuff twice, and continued my discourse in my usual attitude of my body bent forwards, and my forefinger stretched out." In the *silhouette* portrait he is represented as indulging in this habit, and looking, as Colman expresses it, " like an erect, black tadpole, taking snuff."

### CHARLES LAMB AS A SMOKER.

CHARLES LAMB, in the briefest and wittiest autobiography in the language, confessed that he had been "a fierce smoker of tobacco," though he desired at the time of writing to be likened to "a volcano burnt out and emitting only now and then a casual puff." Years before, he had written, " I design to give up smoking, but I have not yet fixed on the equivalent vice," and in a letter to Wordsworth on the occasion of sending him the " Farewell to Tobacco," he says, " Tobacco has been my evening comfort and my morning curse for these five years. I have had it in my head to write this poem for these two years, but tobacco stood in its own light when it gave me headaches that prevented my singing its praises." His "loving foe," his "friendly traitress," the "great plant," as he variously denominates tobacco, seemed to him the cause of that indisposition which Carlyle was inclined to attribute to his "insuperable proclivity to gin." Nevertheless the delights of smoking haunted his imagination to the last. " I once," says the late Mr. John Forster, " heard him express a wish that his last breath might be drawn through a pipe and exhaled in a pun."

----

## A FAREWELL TO TOBACCO.

MAY the Babylonish curse
    Straight confound my stammer-
        ing verse,
If I can a passage see
In this word-perplexity,
Or a fit expression find,
Or a language to my mind
(Still the phrase is wide or scant),
To take leave of thee, Great Plant !
Or in any terms relate
Half my love or half my hate:
For I hate yet love thee so,
That, whichever thing I show,
The plain truth will seem to be
A constrain'd hyperbole,
And the passion to proceed
More from a mistress than a weed.

Sooty retainer to the vine,
Bacchus' black servant, negro-fine ;
Sorcerer, that makest us dote upon
Thy begrimed complexion,
And for thy pernicious sake,
More and greater oaths to break
Than reclaimed lovers take
'Gainst women : thou thy siege dost lay
Much too in the female way,
While thou suck'st the labouring breath
Faster than kisses or than death.

Thou in such a cloud dost bind us,
That our worst foes cannot find us,
And ill fortune, that would thwart us,
Shoots at rovers, shooting at us ;
While each man, through thy heightening
      steam,
Does like a smoking Etna seem,
And all about us does express
(Fancy and wit in richest dress)
A Sicilian fruitfulness.

Thou through such a mist dost show us,
That our best friends do not know us,
And, for those allowed features,
Due to reasonable creatures,
Liken'st us to fell chimeras—
Monsters that, who see us, fear us ;
Worse than Cerberus or Geryon,
Or. who first loved a cloud. Ixion.

Bacchus we know, and we allow
His tipsy rites.   But what art thou,
That but by reflex canst show
What his deity can do,
As the false Egyptain spell
Aped the true Hebrew miracle ?
Some few vapours thou may'st raise,
The weak brain may serve to amaze,
But to the reins and nobler heart
Canst nor life nor heat impart.

Brother of Bacchus, later born,
The old world was sure forlorn
Wanting thee, that aidest more
The god's victories than before
All his panthers, and the brawls
Of his piping Bacchanals.
These, as stale, we disallow,
Or judge of *thee* meant : only thou
His true Indian conquest art ;
And, for ivy round his dart,
The reformed god now weaves
A finer thyrsus of thy leaves.
Scent to match thy rich perfume
Chemic art did ne'er presume
Through her quaint alembic strain,
None so sovereign to the brain.
Nature that did in thee excel,
Framed again no second smell.
Roses, violets, but toys,
For the smaller sort of boys,

Or for greener damsels meant;
Thou art the only manly scent.

Stinking'st of the stinking kind,
Filth of the mouth and fog of the mind
Africa, that brags her foison,
Breeds no such prodigious poison,
Henbane, nightshade, both together,
Hemlock, aconite—

                 Nay, rather,
Plant divine, of rarest virtue;
Blisters on the tongue would hurt you.
'Twas but in a sort I blamed thee,
None e'er prosper'd who defamed thee:
Irony all and feign'd abuse,
Such as perplex'd lovers use
At a need, when, in despair,
To paint forth their fairest fair,
Or in part but to express
That exceeding comeliness
Which their fancies doth so strike,
They borrow language of dislike;
And, instead of Dearest Miss,
Jewel, Honey, Sweetheart, Bliss,
And those forms of old admiring,
Call her Cockatrice and Siren,
Basilisk, and all that's evil,
Witch, Hyena, Mermaid, Devil,
Ethiop, Wench and Blackamoor,
Monkey, Ape, and twenty more:
Friendly Traitress, Loving Foe,—

Not that she is truly so,
But no other way they know
A contentment to express,
Borders so upon recess,
That they do not rightly wot
Whether it be pain or not.

Or as men, constrain'd to part,
With what's nearest to their heart,
While their sorrow's at the height,
Lose discrimination quite,
And their hasty wrath let fall,
To appease their frantic gall,
On the darling thing whatever
Whence they feel it death to sever,
Though it be, as they, perforce,
Guiltless of the sad divorce.

For I must (nor let it grieve thee,
Friendliest of plants, that I must) leave thee.
For thy sake, Tobacco, I,
Would do anything but die,
And but seek to extend my days
Long enough to sing thy praise.
But, as she who once hath been
A king's consort, is a queen
Ever after, nor will bate
Any tittle of her state
Though a widow, or divorced,
So I, from thy converse forced,
The old name and style retain,

A right Katherine of Spain :
And a seat, too, 'mongst the joys
Of the blest Tobacco Boys ;
Where, though I, by sour physician,
Am debarr'd the full fruition
Of thy favours, I may catch
Some collateral sweets, and snatch
Sidelong odours, that give life
Like glances from a neighbour's wife ;
And still live in the by-places
And the suburbs of thy graces ;
And in thy borders take delight
An unconquer'd Canaanite.

*Charles Lamb.*

---

### THE POWER OF SMOKE.

WHAT is this smoking, that it should be considered a crime ?  I believe in my heart that women are jealous of it, as of a rival.  The fact is, that the cigar *is* a rival to the ladies, and their conqueror too.  Do you suppose you will conquer ?  Look over the wide world, and see that your adversary has overcome it. Germany has been puffing for three-score years; France smokes to a man.  Do you think you can keep the enemy out of England ?  Pshaw ! look at his progress. Ask the club-houses.  I, for my part, do not despair to see a bishop lolling out of the Athenæum with a cheroot in his mouth, or, at any rate, a pipe stuck in his shovel hat."—*Thackeray,* "*Fitzboodle Papers.*"

---

## THACKERAY AS A SMOKER.

THACKERAY always began writing with a cigar in his mouth, as one might easily guess from the aroma which pervades his books from "that great unbosomer of secrets." The Earl of Crabs, in the Deuceace Papers, George Fitzboodle and Warrington, are emphatically smoking characters; but who among his types of nineteenth-century men is not drawn with pipe or cigar as the "fragrant companion of his solitude?" The wonder is that he did not so adorn the portraits of his women; yet we remember that he somewhere expresses an Englishman's repugnance to seeing a lady with "a cigar in her face." Thackeray was a real devotee of tobacco, and sacrificed to his idol unremittingly. A lady relates how, long before "Vanity Fair" was thought of, and when he was only studying how to become a painter, and leading a rollicking artist-life in Paris, he would frequently dash into the room

where she was sitting, and say, "Polly,
lend me a franc for cigars." When
Thackeray was busily occupied in pre-
paring his Lectures—which he dictated to
an amanuensis—every morning found him
up and ready to begin work, though he
sometimes was in doubt and difficulty as
to whether he should commence operations sitting or standing, or walking about,
or lying down.   Often he would light a
cigar, and after pacing the room for a few
minutes would put the unsmoked remnant
on the mantelpiece, and resume his work
with increased cheerfulness, as if he had
gathered fresh inspiration from the gentle
odours of "sublime tobacco."

### DICKENS AS A SMOKER.

BOZ used for some few years to indulge in the titillating dust known
as "Irish blackguard;" but the habit
seems to have been artificially induced by
the presentation to him of a silver snuff-
box by his old teacher, a Baptist minister.
In later years he took to cigars, which, if
he did not consume in large quantities
himself, he kept in abundance for his
friends; but a reminiscence of past joys

that "my nose knows" endeared to him
the career of that snuff-box in Douglas
Jerrold's "Story of a Feather," which he
pronounced to be "masterly." When at
Lausanne he saw at an Institution for the
Deaf and Dumb an afflicted boy, whose
lot had been rendered exceptionally hard
by the additional loss of his sight. This
unfortunate, however, was very fond of
smoking, and Dickens arranged to supply
him with cigars during his stay. On re-
visiting the place some seven years later,
he left ten francs to be expended in cigars
for this smoking patient. The director
had tried to revive the lad's recollections
of Dickens, but without the sense of hearing and sight to work upon, it seemed impossible. Dickens, as the thought struck
him, observed, "Ah, if I had only brought
a cigar with me, I think I could have
established my identity." We catch a
glimpse of Dickens as a nicotian again at
Boulogne, smoking a farewell cigar with
Thackeray, whom he met there, the talk
perchance running on the former's ex-
periences of Lady A., a singular character
whose *personnel* included a cigar-box, and
who had made Dickens smoke with her
some weeds made of negrohead, and
powerful enough, according to his account,
to "quell an elephant in six whiffs."

The snuff-box has again to be mentioned in connexion with the popular novelist. The last entry in his note-book (which contained some hints for the work he was engaged on when death took him) ran: " Then, I'll give up snuff, Brobity—an alarming sacrifice—Mr. Brobity's snuff-box—The pawnbroker's account of it." That silver receptacle for " the dust of Virginia," inscribed " to the inimitable Boz," was perhaps in his thoughts at the time.

-------

CHEWING AND SPITTING IN AMERICA.

THE more Dickens saw of the United States, the more he was impressed with " the prevalence of those two odious practices of chewing and expectorating." Washington in particular he stigmatised as the " headquarters of tobacco-tinctured saliva." In his " American Notes " we read that " In the courts of law the judge has his spittoon, the crier his, the warder his, and the prisoner his ; while the jury-men and spectators are provided for as so many men who, in the course of nature, must desire to spit incessantly. In the hospitals the students of medicine are requested by notices upon the wall to eject their tobacco-juice into the boxes provided for that purpose, and not to discolour the stairs. In public buildings visitors are implored through the same agency to squirt the essence of their quids, or 'plugs,' as I have heard them called by gentlemen learned in this kind of sweet-meat, into the national spittoons, and not about the bases of the marble columns. In some parts this custom is inseparably mixed up with every meal and morning call, and with all the transactions of social life." The national spit-boxes were indeed obnoxious to him, and assuredly he had some grounds for his resentment if the following may be accepted as a bare statement of fact. Writing on a canal-boat, on his way to the tobacco plantations at Richmond, he says, "I was obliged this morning to lay my fur coat on the deck, and wipe the half-dried flakes of spittle from it with my handkerchief; and the only surprise seemed to be that I should consider it necessary to do so! When I turned in last night, I put it on a stool beside me, and there it lay, under a cross fire from five men—three opposite, one above. and one below."

### TENNYSON AS A SMOKER.

THE Poet Laureate is a great smoker. He has never, with Charles Lamb, praised " Bacchus' black servant, Negro fine," nor with Byron hymned the delights of " sublime Tobacco;" but he dearly loves the weed for all that. Poet and dweller in the empyrean though he be, he knows nothing of Mr. Ruskin's scorn for those who " pollute the pure air of the morning with cigar-smoke." But he does not affect Havana in any of its varied forms. His joy is in a pipe of genuine Virginia tobacco. A brother poet, who spent a week with him at his country-seat, says that Partagas, Regalias, and Cabanas have no charm for him. He prefers a pipe, and of all pipes in the world the common clay pipe is his choice. His den is at the top of the house. Thither he repairs after breakfast, and in the midst of a sea of books on shelves, tables, chairs and floor, toils away until he is fatigued. These hours of labour are as absolutely sacred as were Richter's. No human being, unless upon an errand of life or death, is allowed to intrude upon him then ; but when his morning's work is done, he is glad to see his friends—sends for them, indeed, or announces by a little bell his readiness to receive them. As soon as they enter, pipes are lighted. Of these pipes he has a great store, mostly presents from admirers and friends. The visitor has his choice, be it a hookah, narghile, meerschaum, or dhudeen. Tennyson is familiar with all grades of smoking tobacco, and the guest may select at will Latakia, Connecticut leaf, Periquo, Lone Jack, Michigan, Killicinick Highlander, or any of the English brands. The poet himself follows the good old plan of his forefathers, from Raleigh downwards. At his feet is a box full of white clay pipes. Filling one of these, he smokes until it is empty, breaks it in twain, and throws the fragments into another box prepared for their reception. Then he pulls another pipe from its straw or wooden enclosure, fills it, lights it, and destroys it as before. He will not smoke a pipe a second time. Meanwhile, high discourse goes on, interrupted not seldom by the poet's reading select passages from the manuscript which is as yet scarcely dry. So the hours are whiled delightfully away until it is time to stroll on the cliffs or dress for dinner.

### A SMOKER IN VENICE.

THE late Earl Russell once gave a large party to which the Poet Laureate was invited, and during the evening his lordship, sauntering up and down his magnificent halls, happened to recognize Tennyson.

"Hau! Mr. Tennyson, how d'ye do? Glad to see you. Hau! you've been travelling in Europe lately, I hear. How did you like Venice, hau? Fine things to be seen in Venice! Did you visit the Bridge of Sighs, hau?"

"Yes."

"And saw all the pictures, hau! and works of art in that wonderful city, did you not, hau?"

"I didn't like Venice!"

"Hau! Indeed! Why not, Mr. Tennyson?"

"They had no good cigars there, my lord; and I left the place in disgust."

---

### COLERIDGE'S FIRST PIPE.

COLERIDGE, soon after he left Cambridge, set off on a tour to the north canvassing for subscriptions for *The*

*Watchman*, a periodical which he was then about to start. One day he found himself at dinner with a tradesman whose interest he wished to secure, and after dinner, the poet was importuned to smoke a pipe with his host and the rest of the company. " I objected," says Coleridge, " both because I was engaged to spend the evening with a minister and his friends, and because I had never smoked except once or twice in my life-time, and then it was herb tobacco mixed with Oronooko. On the assurance, however, that the tobacco was equally mild, and seeing too, that it was of a yellow colour, I took half a pipe, filling the lower half of the bowl with salt. I was soon, however, compelled to resign it, in consequence of a giddiness and distressful feeling in my eyes, which, as I had drunk but a single glass of ale, must, I knew, have been the effect of the tobacco. Soon after, deeming myself recovered, I sallied forth to my engagement; but the walk and the fresh air brought on all the symptoms again, and I had scarcely entered the minister's drawing-room, ere I sank back on the sofa in a sort of swoon rather than sleep. Fortunately, I had found just time enough to inform him of the confused state of my feelings and of the occasion. For here and thus I lay, my face like a wall that is white-washing, deathly pale, and with the cold drops of perspiration running down it from my forehead, while one after another there dropped in the different gentlemen who had been invited to meet and spend the evening with me, to the number of from fifteen to twenty. As the poison of tobacco acts but for a short time, I at length awoke from insensibility, and looked round on the party, my eyes dazzled by the candles which had been lighted in the interim."

Coleridge, however, was afterwards able to surmount the difficulties that are experienced by almost every novice in the art of smoking, for Charles Lamb—that " fierce smoker of tobacco," writing to him at Bristol regretted the loss of his companionship in smoking and drinking egg-hot " in some little smoky room in a pot-house."

***

### RICHARD PORSON.

THE bacchanalian habits of the celebrated Greek scholar, Porson, are well known. He would often sally forth from his den in the Temple, after a week of unremitting labour, for a bout of dissipation, and consume at a single sitting, prodigious quantities of wine and tobacco. Mr. Gordon was once favoured with his company (he had been invited to dinner) for six and thirty hours. During this *sederunt*, it was computed that Porson dispatched a bottle of alcohol, two bottles of Trinity ale, and six of claret, besides much of the lighter sort of wines. He also emptied a half-pound canister of snuff, and on the first night smoked a bundle of cigars. "Previous to this exhibition," wrote his host many years afterwards, "I had always considered the powers of man as limited."

———

## CRUIKSHANK AND TOBACCO.

CRUIKSHANK'S portrait of himself (in the "Table Book"), meerschaum in mouth, with a little 'King Charles' on his knee, is a charming study, and moreover, establishes the fact that at one period at least, of his life, George was a sedulous smoker. During his last twenty years, however, he was as resolute in his denunciation of the weed as of the wine-cup. Only to a few very dearly-prized literary friends would he show himself tolerant in the matter of tobacco. "I want you to give up drinking and smoking," he would say, "and you tell me that if you don't smoke you can't write. Now, I'll meet you half-way. Give up the drink, and you may smoke—just a little."

---

### MR. JAMES PAYN.

MR. James Payn, the novelist, puffs eternally at a pipe of Latakia. Even while at work he smokes persistently, still at that Latakia which the doctors once told him would "kill the strongest man in ten years," but which he has smoked for a quarter of a century with impunity. Shortly after the evening post comes in, the last pipe is lighted, and at ten o'clock the household is wrapped in slumber.

---

### MR. SWINBURNE ON RALEIGH.

AN amusing story is told of the most eminent of the "fleshly school" of poets. One day at the Arts Club, after going from room to room in the vain hope of finding a clear atmosphere to write in,

Mr. Swinburne delivered himself of the following :

" James the First was a knave, a tyrant, a fool, a liar, a coward. But I love him, I worship him, because he slit the throat of that blackguard Raleigh, who invented this filthy smoking."

---

## THE ANTI-TOBACCO PARTY.

THERE has always existed a party devoted to the expulsion of the " Divine Plant" from our midst. Voltaire, Rousseau and Mirabeau have each in turn thundered forth anathemas against tobacco. " The nation that smokes perishes," said Charles Fourier, in a sentence as terse as it was dogmatic and untenable, when viewed in the light of the federation into one mighty Empire of the numerous German States, each impotent in itself, yet forming one resistless whole. The following, attributed to Stendhal, is certainly not so utterly at variance with established fact. " If the Turk wears his fatalism impressed upon his features, if the German fritters away his existence in an ideal dreamland, if the Spaniard sleeps the sleep of the somnambulist, if in short, the Frenchman

E

already lets his steadfast eye waver, the chibouque, pipe, cigar, and cigarette should bear the blame."

––––––

"THIS INDIAN WEED NOW WITHERED QUITE."

The following "moral" song is a modern adaptation of a quaint piece originally published in 1631, in a volume entitled *The Soules Solace*, by Thomas Jenner :—

THIS Indian weed—now wither'd
      quite,
Though green at noon—cut down at
    night,
      Shews thy decay,
      All flesh is hay—
Thus think and smoke tobacco.

The pipe so lily white and weak
Doth thus thy mortal state bespeak,
      Thou art e'en such
      Gone with a touch !—
Thus think and smoke tobacco.

And when the smoke ascends on high
Then dost thou see the vanity
      Of worldly stuff
      Gone with a puff !—
Thus think and smoke tobacco.

And when the pipe grows foul within,
Think of thy soul begrimed with sin ;
    For then the fire
    It does require !—
Thus think and smoke tobacco.

And seest thou the ashes cast away,
Then to thyself thou mayest say
    That to the dust
    Return thou must !—
Thus think and smoke tobacco.

----

### DR. ABERNETHY ON SNUFF-TAKING.

ONE day a gentleman asked Dr. Abernethy if the moderate use of snuff would injure the brain.

"No, sir," answered the doctor immediately, "for no man with an ounce of brain would ever dream of using it !"

----

### ABERNETHY AND A SMOKING PATIENT.

A YOUNG man once consulted this famous doctor. After interrogating the patient upon his life and habits, Abernethy was puzzled to account for the state in which he found the sufferer. Suddenly a thought struck him. "Do you expectorate, sir?" he inquired. The patient replied that since he smoked a good deal spitting had become habitual with him. "Ah! that need not cause you to expectorate," mused the doctor. "Well, well," he resumed, "I'll just take time to think over your case; you can call on me to-morrow morning, at eleven o'clock, for a prescription." The following morning Dr. Abernethy's patient punctually made his appearance. "I'm very sorry, sir, but I have a pressing engagement just now; if you'll step upstairs into my drawing-room and wait for half-an-hour, you'll find a box of Colorados to amuse yourself with."

"Well, now, what do you think of my cigars?" said Abernethy, when in the course of an hour he came into the room in which his patient awaited him—a room, be it said, luxuriously furnished with every possible convenience except that of a spittoon. "I enjoyed the first so much that I could not help taking a second." "But where then," said Dr. A., prying curiously under the table and inside the grate, "have you been spitting?" "Good gracious, doctor, what can you be thinking of, to imagine that in such a place I should do otherwise than swallow my spittle?" "Pay me my fee," said the doctor, "and go, and remember! never say you cannot smoke without spitting. That is your sole complaint!"

---

### TOBACCO AND THE PLAGUE.

WHILST the great Plague raged in London, tobacco was recommended by the faculty, and generally taken as a preventive against infection. Pepys records the following on the 7th of June, 1665. "The hottest day that ever I felt in my life. This day, much against my will, I did in Drury Lane see two or three houses marked with a red cross upon the doors, and 'Lord have mercy upon us!' writ there; which was a sad sight to me, being the first of the kind, that to my remembrance, I ever saw. It put me into an ill conception of myself and my smell, so that I was forced to buy some roll tobacco to smell and chew, which took away the apprehension." Further, it was popularly reported that no tobacconists or their households were afflicted by the plague. Physicians who visited the sick took it very freely; the men who went round with the dead carts had their pipes continually alight. This gave tobacco a new popularity, and it again took the high medical position accorded to it by the physicians of the French Court."

---

## THE GREATEST TOBACCO-STOPPER IN ALL ENGLAND.

DR. PARR'S particular fondness for smoking was so well-known, that wherever he dined, he was always indulged with a pipe. Even George IV., when the worthy Grecian was his guest at Carlton House, graciously provided him with a smoking-room, and the company of Colonel C—, in order that he might suffer no inconvenience. "I don't like to be smoked myself, doctor," said the royal wit, "but I am anxious that your pipe should not be put out." One day Dr. Parr was to dine at the house of Mr. ——, who previously informed his wife of the doctor's passion for his pipe. The lady was much mortified by this intimation, and with warmth said, "I tell you what, Mr. ——, I don't care a fig for Dr. Parr's Greek ; he shan't smoke here."

"My dear," replied the husband, " he

must smoke ; he is allowed to do so every-where." "Excuse me, Mr. ——, he shall not smoke here ;—leave it to me, my dear, I'll manage it."

The doctor came, a splendid dinner was served ; the Grecian was very brilliant, and immediately after the repast called for pipes.

"Pipes !" screamed the lady. "Pipes ! for what purpose ? " "Why to smoke, madam ! " "Oh ! my dear doctor, I can't have pipes here. You'll spoil my room : my curtains will smell of tobacco for a week." "Not smoke ? " exclaimed the astonished and offended doctor. " Why, madam, I have smoked in better houses." "Perhaps so, sir," replied the lady with dignity, adding with firmness, " I shall be most happy to show you the rites of hospitality ; but you cannot be allowed to smoke."

" Then, madam," said Dr. Parr, look-ing at her *ample* person, " then, madam, I must say, madam,"——

" Sir, sir ! are you going to be rude ? "

" I must say, madam," he continued, "you are the *greatest* tobacco-stopper in all England."

———

## DR. RICHARDSON ON TOBACCO.

D R. RICHARDSON, the would-be founder of a modern hygienic Utopia, observes with regard to this subject, " In an adult man who is tolerant of tobacco, moderate smoking, say to the extent of three clean pipes of the milder forms of pure tobacco, in twenty-four hours, does no great harm. It somewhat stops waste and soothes. The ground on which tobacco holds so firm a footing is, that of nearly every luxury it is the least injurious. It is innocuous as compared with alcohol ; it does infinitely less harm than opium ; it is in no sense worse than *tea ;* and by the side of high living altogether, it contrasts most favourably ; a thorough smoker is never a glutton. It brings quiet to the overworn body and restless mind in the poor savage from whom it was derived, killing wearisome, lingering time. The overwrought man discovers in it a quietus for his exhaustion, which, having once tasted, he rarely forgets, but asks for again and again. Tobacco will hold its place with this credit to itself, that, bad as it is, it prevents the introduction of agents that would be infinitely worse."

## ADVICE TO SMOKERS.

IF you will not give up this habit of smoking from motives of economy, from a sense of its uncleanness, from its making your breath smell bad and your clothes filthy, from its polluting your hands and your house, and driving women and men from you who do not smoke, I dare not, as a physiologist or a statist, tell you that there exists any proof of its injurious influence when used in moderation. I know how difficult it is to define that word "moderation;" and yet, in my heart, I believe that every one of you has an internal monitor that will guide you to the true explanation of it in your own case. The first symptoms of giddiness, of sickness, of palpitation, of weakness, of indolence, of uneasiness, whilst smoking, should induce you to lay it aside. These are the physiological indications of its disagreement, which, if you neglect, you may find increase upon you, and seriously embarrass your health.—*Dr. Lankester.*

## SOME STRANGE SMOKERS.

THERE are some strange nicotian practices, an account of which may prove interesting as showing the absolute and universal sway of tobacco.

The Negritos, in Luzon (one of the Philippines) scarcely ever stop smoking cigars, of which it is the lighted end that they place in their mouths. The Hottentots barter their wives for tobacco, and when they cannot obtain it, fill their pipes with a substitute, consisting of the dried excrement of the elephant or rhinoceros. In the snowy regions of the Himalaya, tiny smoking tunnels are made in the frozen snow, at one end of which is placed some tobacco, along with a piece of burning charcoal, while to the other the mountaineers place their mouths, and lying on their stomachs, inhale the smoke of the glowing weed. The Patagonian lights a pipe, throws himself down with his face toward the ground, and swallows several mouthfuls of smoke in a manner which produces a kind of intoxication, lasting for several minutes. The inhabitants of the Cook peninsula in Australia are passionate smokers. Their pipe—a bamboo three and a half feet long and four inches in diameter—passes round the company after one of the persons present has filled it with smoke from a tube.

The noses of the Moschanas, a weak and enervated tribe in Africa, are often seen disfigured by the excessive consumption of snuff. The people sometimes cram their nostrils so full that the mass has to be dug out again with small iron or ivory spoons. The Wadschidschi, dwelling by the banks of the Taganyika Lake, neither chew nor snuff nor smoke their tobacco, but carrying it in a small vessel, the savage pours water upon it and presses out the juice, with which he contrives to fill both nostrils, keeping it there by means of wooden pegs. The Kaffirs, who cannot get snuff as fine and as pungent as they wish, rub the already prepared mass between stones, and mix it with a kind of pepper and some ashes. The blacks in Dscnesire mix their tobacco with water and natron, so as to form a kind of pap, which they call bucka. They take a mouthful, and roll it about for a time with their tongue. There are regular bucka parties given. In Paraguay it is chiefly the women who chew ; and travellers have often described their emotions when on entering a house, a lady dressed in satin, and adorned with precious stones, comes toward them, and, before holding out her mouth to be kissed, as the usual welcome, pulls the beloved tobacco quid from her cheek pouch.

It is calculated that in Virginia, Carolina, Georgia and Alabama, there are at least 100,000 "tobacco-dippers," as they are called, who consume a great quantity of snuff in the following manner. The dippers take a small stick, moisten it, dip it into the snuff and rub it into the gaps between their teeth, and there let the dark brown powder remain till it has lost its pungency. Others hold the stick covered with tobacco in their mouths, and suck it as children suck a stick of barley-sugar. Some South-American tribes actually eat the tobacco cut into small pieces. Finally, there is a traveller's story told of certain Esquimaux tribes that, if true, is not a little remarkable. When a stranger arrives in Greenland, it is said that he finds himself immediately surrounded by a multitude of natives, who ask his permission to drink that empyreumatic oil which remains in the stem of his pipe. And it is stated that the Greenlanders smoke for no other purpose than to enjoy afterwards the swallowing of that acrid and poisonous matter which is so disgusting to us.

## THE ETYMOLOGY OF TOBACCO.

I MUST beg leave to dissent from somebody who has written very unfavourably of smoking tobacco, as bad for the lungs, &c. If he mean to say that the frequent practice of smoking, and such a habit of doing it as that a man cannot be happy without it, is a prejudicial thing, I agree with him. Tobacco-smoke is a stimulant, and therefore the frequent and immoderate use of it must tend to weaken the constitution in the same way, though in a much smaller degree, that dram-drinking, or anything else that excites the nervous system, does. But against the moderate and occasional use of it there exists no rational objection. It is a valuable article in medicine. I have known much good from it in various cases, and have myself been recovered by it, at times, from a languor which neither company nor wine was able to dissipate. Although, therefore, I shall not decide on the justness of the etymology, I must clearly assent to the truth of the fact asserted by that critic who found its name to be derived from three Hebrew

words which, if I recollect aright, were
*Tob*-BONUS, *Ach*-FUMUS, *A*-EJUS, " Good is
the smoke thereof."—*Gentleman's Maga-
zine* (*January*, 1788), *vol. lviii., p.* 34.

————

### THE SNUFF CALLED IRISH BLACKGUARD.

THIS snuff unquestionably derived its
first name from that of its maker,
Lundy Foot, whose place of business was
opposite Essex Bridge, Dublin.    Tradition
is, however, by no means clear or decisive
as to the origin of its alternative name.
The most generally received version of the
story is that the man who was in charge
of the kiln in which the snuff was drying
went to sleep and let the precious " titillating dust " burn !   His enraged master
put the " charred remains " into a tub
which stood at the door of the shop, in
order that all the poor passers-by might
help themselves to a pinch and thus rid
him of the waste.    Lundy Foot then
either applied the name " Irish Blackguard " to the snuff, with reference to the
passers by who took their gratuitous pinch,

or with regard to the carelessness of his own servant. Another version is that a large fire having taken place at the warehouse of a rival tobacconist, Lundy Foot bought up some of his damaged stock for a mere song, with the intention of selling it very cheaply to his poorer customers. The Irish palate was, however, so tickled with the particular pungency of this mixture, that its use spread among all classes, and crept into the Castle itself, where it was in great request. So that when the "salvage stock" was exhausted there arose a loud and imperious cry for more "Irish Blackguard," a demand which Foot took good care to supply. It is a touching tribute to the latent goodness in human nature that Foot never forgot the poor snuffers who had so helped to noise abroad the fame of his snuff, and had thus so wonderfully increased his "takings;" for we are told that he ever after placed a keg of "Irish Blackguard" at his door, from which the poor might regale their olfactory nerves "free, gratis, and for nothing."

---

### A SNUFF-MAKER'S SIGN.

OBJECTS connected with various trades, with the crown above them, were very common as shop-signs. The Crown and Rasp occurs as the sign of Fribourg and Treyer, tobacconists in 1781 at the upper end of Pall Mall, near the Haymarket, and is still to be seen on the façade of their house. The oldest form of taking snuff was to scrape it with a rasp from the dry rolled leaves of the tobacco plant ; the powder was then placed on the back of the hand and so snuffed up ; hence the name of *râpé* (rasped) for a kind of snuff, and the common tobacconist's sign of La Carotte d'Or (the golden root or plug), in France. The rasps for this purpose were carried in the waistcoat pocket, and soon became articles of luxury, being carved in ivory and variously enriched. Some of them, in ivory and inlaid wood, may be seen at the Hôtel Cluny in Paris, and an engraving of such an object occurs in "Archæologia" (vol. xiii.). One of the first snuff-boxes was the so called *râpé*, or *grivoise* box, at the back of which was a little space for a piece of the plug, whilst a small iron rasp was contained in the middle. When a pinch was wanted, the plug was drawn a few times over the iron rasp, and so the snuff was produced and could be offered to a friend with much more grace than under the above-mentioned process with the pocket grater.

————

## MR. SALA'S CIGAR-SHOP.

M R. G. A. Sala writes:—"There used some years ago to be a little tobacconist's shop, somewhere between Pall Mall and Duncannon-street, by the sign of the Morro Castle. It was such a little shop, and it smelt so strongly of cedar and of the Indian weed, that itself was not unlike a cigar-box. Here I used to think a threepenny cigar about the greatest luxury in which a young man of pleasure could indulge; but a luxury only to be ventured upon at the occurrence of solemn festivals, and when the treasures of the mines of Potosi, to the extent of a few shillings, lay loose in one's waistcoat-pocket. There *were* threepenny cigars in those days, and they were delicious. I am afraid that the manufacture has ceased, or that the threepennies have lost their flavour, for Ensign and Lieutenant Dickey-

strap, of the Guards, declares that you
cannot get anything fit to smoke under
ninepence, and that a really tolerable
'weed' will 'stand you in' eighteenpence.
Prince Fortunatus, they say, gives half-a
crown apiece for his Regalias.

The Morro Castle, however, did a very
modest but, I believe, remunerative business in cigars at from threepence to six-
pence each.   Well do I remember courtly
old Mr. Alcachofado, the proprietor of the
Morro—always in the same well-buttoned
frock-coat, always with the same tall shiny
hat with the broad turned-up brim—always
puffing at, apparently, the same stump of
a choice Londres.   It was well worth
while laying out threepence at the Morro
Castle ; for, in consideration of that
modest investment, you were treated, for
at least five minutes, like a peer of the
realm.   Mr. Alcachofado himself selected
your cigar, and if you approved of it,
snipped off the end in a little patent
machine, and presented it to you with a
grave bow.   You proposed to light it ;
but this Mr. Alcachofado would by no
means permit.   He drew a splint from a
stack in a japanned stand, kindled it at
the gas-jet, and with another bow handed
it to you.   If you wished to fill the heart
of Mr. Alcachofado with anguish, and to

pass in his eyes for a person of the very
worst breeding, you would, when the splint
had served your turn, cast it on the floor,
and trample it underfoot. I have seen the
proprietor of the Morro glare at people
who did this, as though he-would have
dearly liked to take off his curly-brimmed
hat and fling it at their heads. Regular
customers knew well the etiquette of the
Morro, which was gently to blow out the
tiny flame of the splint, and place it hori-
zontally on the top of the fasces in the
japanned tin box. Then *you* bowed to
Mr. Alcachofado, and *he* bowed in return ;
and, taking a seat, if you liked, on a huge
cigar chest, you proceeded to smoke the
calumet of peace. Did I say that for five
minutes you would be treated like a noble-
man ? You might softly kick your heels,
and meditate on the transitory nature of
earthly things, in that snug little shop, for
nearly half an hour. Threepenny cigars
lasted five-and-twenty minutes in those
days. Austere personages of aristocratic
mien patronised Mr. Alcachofado. They
looked like County Members, Masters in
Chancery, Charity Commissioners. They
looked as though they belonged to Clubs.
They called the proprietor Alcatchany-
thing, without the Mr. He was gravely
courteous to them. but not more so than

to humbler patrons. I remember that he
always took in the second edition of the
*Globe.* I have, in my time, bespoken it,
I think, not without fear and trembling,
from a Baronet. They were affable creatures, those exalted ones, and talked
sedate commonplaces about the House,
and the crops, and the revenue, until I
used to fancy I had land and beeves and a
stake in the country. There was only one
absolutely haughty customer. He wore a
spencer and gaiters, and sometimes swore.
He smoked a costlier cigar than the ordinary race of puffers; and one had to
rise from the big cigar-chest while Mr.
Alcachofado, a shining bunch of keys in
hand, like a discreet sacristan, unlocked
this treasure-coffer, and produced regalias
of price. Yet even this haughty man in
the spencer gave me a bow once when I
brushed by him in the lobby of the House,
where I had been waiting two hours and
a quarter, on a night when Sir Robert Peel
was ' up,' in the vain hope of getting into
the strangers' gallery, with an Irish member's order.

The haughty man thought he knew me.
I felt so proud that I had my hair cut the
very next day, and determined, like Mr.
Pepys, to ' go more like myself.' A
grave company we were at Mr. Alcacho-

fado's. Now and then, on Opera nights,
dandies in evening dress would stroll
in to smoke a cigarette. There was
great scandal one evening—it was Grisi's
benefit—when a tall young man, with a
white cravat and a tawny moustache,
ordered Mr. Alcachofado to 'open him a
bottle of soda and look sharp.' Those
were his very words. There was a com-
motion among the customers. Soda-water !
Was this a tobacconist's and fancy sta-
tioner's in the Clapham-road? As well
might you have asked the beadle of St.
George's, Hanover-square, for hot whiskey-
toddy, between psalm and sermon.

Mr. Alcachofado, under the circumstances, was calm. He gave the tall young
desperado one look, to wither him, and
in slow and measured accents, not devoid
of a touch of sarcasm, replied, 'I sell
neither soda-water, nor ginger-beer, nor
walking-sticks, nor penny valentines, sir.'
The customers grimly chuckled at this
overwhelming rebuke. There was nothing
left for the tall young man but to with-
draw ; but, as I was nearest the door, I
am constrained to state that as he lounged
out he remarked that the 'old guy', meaning Mr Alcachofado, 'seemed doosid
crusty.' "

*Under the Sun, pp.* 34-37.

DEATH OF THE "YARD OF CLAY."

WHILE I speak of lights and smoke, says Mr. Sala in "Household Words," another thing departed comes before me. There is no such thing as a pipe of tobacco, now-a-days, sir. I see English gentlemen going about smoking black abominations, like Irish apple-women. I hear of Milo's, Burns' cutty pipes, Narghiles, Chiboucks, Meerschaums, Hookahs, water-pipes, straw-pipes, and a host of other inventions for emitting the fumes of tobacco. But where, sir, is the old original Alderman's pipe? the churchwarden's pipe? the unadulterated "yard of clay?" A man was wont to moisten the stem carefully with beer ere he put it to his lips ; when once it was alight, however, it kept alight : a man could sit behind *that* pipe ; but can he sit behind the miserable figments they call pipes in these days? The yard of clay is departed. A dim shadow of it lingers sometimes in the parlours of old City taverns; I met with it once in the Bull Ring at Birmingham : I have heard of it in Chester; but in its entirety, as a popular, acknowledged pipe, it must be numbered with the things that were.

## A PRODIGIOUS SMOKER.

IN June, 1860, there died at Ath, in Belgium, an unrivalled beer-drinker and smoker. It is estimated that between the ages of eighteen and ninety-one, he drank more than 22,000 gallons of beer and consumed upwards of four tons of tobacco. This bold smoker appears to have undertaken the task of putting to confusion the enemies of the fragrant weed.

----

## A PROFESSOR OF SMOKING.

" IF this city, or the suburbs of the same, do afford any young gentleman of the first, second, or third head, more or less, whose friends are but lately deceased, and whose lands are but new come into his hands, that, to be as exactly qualified as the best of our ordinary gallants are, is affected to entertain the most gentlemanlike use of Tobacco; as first, to give it the most exquisite perfume ; then, to know all the delicate, sweet forms for the assumption of it ; as also the rare corollary and practice of the Cuban ebolition, euripus, and whiff, which he shall receive. or take in here at Lon-

don, and evaporate at Uxbridge, or
farther, if it please him.   If there be any
such generous spirit, that is truly ena-
moured of these good faculties; may it
please him, but by a note of his hand to
specify the place or ordinary where he
uses to eat and lie ; and most sweet atten-
dance, with Tobacco and pipes of the
best sort, shall be ministered.   *Stet,
quæso, candide Lector.*"

This placard was hung in St. Paul's (in
1599).   The cathedral was then held to
be the most fashionable promenade of
the day, and was therefore the most suitable place for the impudent and pedantic
advertisement of Signor Whiffe.

----

## TOBACCO IN TIME OF WAR.

DR. RUSSELL tells a good story of
French wit, and Prussian practica-
lity.   There is a great tobacco manufactory in Nancy, on which the Prussians
descended with irresistible *élan.*   Cigars
and tobacco, which they consider a necessary of life, were seized at once ; and all
that was needed to be done, was to carry
the treasure off.   The director made his

bow, took perhaps a pinch of snuff, and said with another bow,

"Apparently, M. le Colonel has forgotten something."

"What?"

"There is a quantity of tobacco in leaf which he has not been good enough to notice. Will he not kindly take charge of it?"

"Oh, dear no!" said the Prussian; "set to work at once and manufacture it. *We* will pay the work-people."

———

### AGES ATTAINED BY GREAT SMOKERS.

INVETERATE smokers have reached very great ages. Hobbes, who smoked twelve pipes a-day at Chatsworth, attained the age of 92; Izaak Walton, 90; Dr Parr, 78—all devoted lovers of the pipe; and Dr. Isaac Barrow called tobacco his "panpharmacon."

In 1769, died Abraham Favrot, a Swiss baker, aged 104; to the last he walked firmly, read without spectacles, and always had a pipe in his mouth.

In 1845, died Pheasy Molly, of Buxton, Derbyshire, aged 96; she was burnt to

F

death, her clothes becoming ignited whilst lighting her pipe at the fire.

In 1856, there died at Wellbury, North Riding of Yorkshire, Jane Garbutt, aged 110; she retained her faculties and enjoyed her pipe to the last; she had smoked "very nigh a hundred years."

Wadd, in his *Comments on Corpulency*, mentions an aged Effendi, "whose back was bent like a bow, and who was in the habit of taking daily four ounces of rice, thirty cups of coffee, and three grains of opium, besides smoking sixty pipes of tobacco."

Mr. Chatto, in his amusing *Paper of Tobacco*, relates that some time ago there was living at Hildhausen, in Silesia, a certain Heinrich Hartz, aged 142, who had been a tobacco-taker from his youth, and still continued to smoke a pipe or two every day.

Although the lovers of smoking have pressed Old Parr into their evidence, in its favour, they must yield to the authority of Taylor, the Water-Poet, who in his *Old, Old very Old man; or the Age and Life of Thomas Parr*, says :—

> " He had but little time to waste,
> Or at the ale-house, huff-cap ale to taste ;
> Nor did he ever hunt a tavern fox ;
> Ne'er knew a coach. *tobacco.* etc."

### A MAIDEN'S WISH.

THE following is derived from a New York paper. "A thoughtful girl says, that when she dies she desires to have tobacco planted over her grave, that the weed nourished by her dust, may be chewed by her bereaved lovers." Steinmetz has suggested the lines given below as a suitable epitaph for this tobacco-loving maiden :—

> " Let no cold marble o'er my body rise,
> But only earth above and sunny skies.
> Thus would I lowly lie in peaceful rest,
> Nursing the Herb Divine, from out my breast.
> Green let it grow above this clay of mine,
> Deriving strength from strength that I resign.
> So in the days to come, when I'm beyond
> This fickle life, will come my lovers fond,
> And gazing on the plant, their grief restrain
> In whispering, 'Lo! dear Anna blooms again!' "

### " THOSE DREADFUL CIGARS."

THE only instance of embarrassment I could not overcome, said the temperance advocate, Mr. John B. Gough, occurred many years ago. It was my own fault, and proved a sharp lesson to me. I was engaged to address a large number of children in the afternoon, the meeting to be held on the lawn back of the Baptist church in Providence, N. J.   In the forenoon a friend met me, and said :—

"I have some first-rate cigars, will you take a few?"

"No, I thank you."

"Do take half-a-dozen."

"I have nowhere to put them."

"You can put half-a-dozen in your cap."

I wore a cap in those days, and I put the cigars into it, and at the appointed time I went to the meeting.   I ascended the platform and faced an audience of more than two thousand children.   As it was out of door, I kept my cap on, for fear of taking cold, and I forgot all about the cigars.   Towards the close of my speech I became much in earnest, and after warning the boys against bad company, bad habits, and the saloons, I said :

"Now boys, let us give three rousing cheers for temperance and for cold water. Now, then, three cheers.   Hurrah!"

And taking off my cap, I waved it most vigorously, when away went the cigars right into the midst of the audience.

The remaining cheers were very faint,

and were nearly drowned in the laughter of the crowd.

I was mortified and ashamed, and should have been relieved, could I have sunk through the platform out of sight. My feelings were still more aggravated by a boy coming up the steps of the platform with one of those dreadful cigars, saying :

"Here's one of your cigars, Mr. Gough."

————

## HOW TO TAKE A PINCH OF SNUFF.

STEINMETZ says :—" The true snuff-taker, who is bold in his propensities, always has a large wooden snuff-box, which he opens with a crash, and which he flourishes about him, with an air of satisfaction and pride. He takes a pinch with three fingers, and then, bringing the whole upon his thumb, he sniffs it up with that lusty pleasure with which a rustic smacks a kiss upon the round and ruddy cheek of his sweetheart.

The true artistic method, however, of 'taking a pinch' consists of twelve operations :—

1. Take the snuff-box with your right hand.

2. Pass the snuff-box to your left hand.

3. Rap the snuff-box.

4. Open the snuff-box.

5. Present the box to the company.

6. Receive it after going the round.

7. Gather up the snuff in the box by striking the side with the middle and forefinger.

8. Take up a pinch with the right hand.

9. Keep the snuff a moment or two between the fingers before carrying it to the nose.

10. Put the snuff to your nose.

11. Sniff it in with precision by both nostrils, and without any grimace.

12. Shut the snuff-box, sneeze, spit, and wipe your nose."

————

### THE TOBACCO PLANT.

"TOBACCO, or henbane of Peru, hath very great stalks of the bigness of a child's arm, growing in fertile and well-dunged ground seven or eight feet high, dividing itself in sundry branches of great length, whereon are placed in most comely order very fair, long leaves, broad, smooth, and sharp-pointed ; soft and of a light

green colour; so fastened about the stalk
that they seem to embrace and compass it
about. The flowers grow at the top of
the stalks, in shape like a bell-flower,
somewhat long and cornered; hollow
within, of a light carnation colour, tending
to whiteness towards the brims. The seed
is contained in long, sharp-pointed cods,
or seed vessels, like unto the seed of
yellow henbane, but somewhat smaller
and browner of colour. The root is great,
thick, and of a woody substance, with
some thready strings annexed thereunto."
—*Gerard's Herball.* 1636.

---

## FATE OF AN EARLY SMOKER.

THE well-known anecdote of Raleigh's
servant drenching him with beer
on seeing him as he supposed on fire,
originated with the famous jester, Dick
Tarlton, who died in 1588. The tale is
told how Tarlton "took tobacco at the
first coming up of it, as other gentlemen
used, more for fashion's sake than otherwise; and, being in a room, sat between
two men overcome with wine, and they
never seeing the like, wondered at it, and
seeing the vapour come out of Tarlton's

nose, cried out, *Fire ! fire !* and threw a
cup of wine in his face.   ' Make no more
stir,' quoth Tarlton, ' the fire is quenched ;
if the sheriffs come it will turn a fine, as
the custom is.'   And *drinking* that again,
 Fie !' said the other, 'what a stink it makes ;
I am almost poisoned.'   ' If it offend,'
quoth Tarlton, ' let's every one take a
little of the smell, and so the savour will
quickly go ;'  but, as the story abruptly
concludes, " *tobacco whiffs made them leave
him to pay all.*"

A later version of the story is the following :—" I remember a pretty jest of tobacco," says Rich (1619), " which was this :
A certain Welchman coming newly to
London, and beholding one to take
tobacco, never seeing the like before,
and not knowing the manner of it, but
perceiving him vent smoke so fast, and
supposing his inward parts to be on fire,
cried out, ' O Jhesu, Jhesu, man, for the
passion of Cod, hold ; for by Cod's splud
ty snowt's on fire ;' and having a bowl of
beer in his hand, threw it at the other's
face, to quench his smoking nose."

## ADDING INSULT TO INJURY.

A SPECTATOR in the pit at the Opera felt a certain pressure upon his coat-pocket, of the aim and object of which he was but too well aware. "You have taken my snuff-box," said he quickly but cautiously to an individual, of very suspicious aspect, who was standing next him. " Return it to me, or I—" "Don't make a noise, I beseech you; pray don't ruin me. Here, take back your snuff-box," added the shabby customer in a low voice, at the same time holding his coat-pocket wide open, into which the too confiding owner of the missing *tabatière* thrust his hand. The rogue immediately caught hold of it and cried "Thief! thief!" and showed the imprisoned hand to the spectators. The veritable owner of the snuff-box was forthwith arrested, but, of course, soon proved his innocence. In the meantime, however, both snuff-box and accuser had disappeared!

TOM BROWN'S EXHORTATORY LETTER TO
AN ANCIENT DAME THAT SMOKED
TOBACCO.

" THOUGH the ill-natured world censures you for smoking, yet would
I advise you, madam, not to part with so
innocent a diversion.    In the first place,
it is healthful; and, as Galen rightly
observes, is a sovereign remedy for the
toothache, the constant persecutor of old
ladies.    Secondly, tobacco, though it be
an heathenish word, is a great help to
Christian meditations, which is the reason,
I suppose, that recommends it to your
parsons, the generality of whom can no
more write a sermon without a pipe in
their mouths, than a Concordance in their
hands ; besides, every pipe you break may
serve to put you in mind upon what slender
accidents man's life depends.    I knew a
dissenting minister who on fast-days used
to mortify upon a rump of beef, because
it put him, as he said, in mind that all
flesh was grass ; but I am sure much more
is to be learnt from tobacco.    It may
instruct you that riches, beauty, and all
the glories of the world, vanish like a
vapour.    Thirdly, it is a pretty play-thing.

Fourthly, and lastly, it is fashionable—at least, 'tis in a fair way of becoming so." (*Circa* 1700.)

———

### THE SNUFF-TAKER.

(*By the Rev. W. King, of Mallow,* 1788.)

> "——Before I budge an inch
> I hail Aurora with a pinch ;
> After three cups of morning tea
> A pinch most grateful is to me ;
> If then by chance the post arrive,
> My fingers still the deeper dive.
> When gallant Nelson gains his point,
> I sink in deep to middle joint ;
> And soon as e'er the work he clinches,
> Oh, then I take the pinch of pinches !
> But if our heroes chance to fail,
> I seldom go beyond the nail.
> If I on ancient classics pore,
> Or turn their learned pages o'er,
> I take a pinch at every pause,
> A tribute of my just applause,
> Whene'er I dip in page historic,
> Or pass an hour in wit with Yorick,
> I relish more each paragraph
> If season'd with a pinch and laugh.
> Or if discussing subjects curious,

I revel in a pinch luxurious ;
E'en joyous friends and claret rosy,
Insipid are *sans* pinches cosy.
Whate'er I do, where'er I be,
My social box attends on me ;
It warms my nose in winter's snow,
Refreshes midst midsummer's glow ;
Of hunger sharp it blunts the edge,
And softens grief, as some allege.
Thus, eased of care or any stir,
I broach my freshest canister ;
And freed from trouble, grief, or panic,
I pinch away in snuff balsamic ;
For rich or poor, in peace or strife,
It smoothes the rugged path of life."

----

## TOBACCO IN NORTH AMERICA.

MR. FAIRHOLT gives the following version of the Indian tradition as to its first appearance in North America. " A Swedish minister who took occasion to inform the chiefs of the Susquehannah Indians, in a kind of sermon, of the principal historical facts on which the Christian religion is founded, and particularly the fall of our first parents, was thus answered by an old Indian orator :—" What you have told us is very good; we thank you for

coming so far to tell us those things you
have heard from your mothers ; in return
we will tell you what we have heard from
ours. In the beginning we had only flesh
of animals to eat ; and if they failed, we
starved. Two of our hunters having killed
a deer, and broiled a part of it, saw a young
woman descend from the clouds, and seat
herself on a hill hard by. Said one to the
other, ' It is a spirit, perhaps, that has
smelt our venison ; let us offer some of it
to her.' They accordingly gave her the
tongue. She was pleased with its flavour,
and said : ' Your kindness shall be re-
warded ; come here thirteen moons hence,
and you shall find it.' They did so, and
found, where her right hand had touched
the ground, maize growing ; where her left
hand had been, kidney-beans ; and where
she had sat, they found *Tobacco*."

We are told that the Indians were so constant in their devotion to the pipe, that they
used it as Europeans use a watch, and in
reckoning the time anything occupied,
would say, " I was one pipe (of time) about
it." When circumstances have prevented
him from procuring an ordinary pipe, the
Indian has been known to dig a small hole
in the ground, light his tobacco in it, and
draw the smoke through a reed. If they
fall short of provisions when on a long

journey, they mix the juice of tobacco with powdered shells, in the form of little balls which they keep in their mouths, and the gradual solution of which serves to counteract the uneasy craving of the stomach.

---

### NATIONAL CHARACTERISTICS.

AN Englishman and a Frenchman were travelling together in a diligence, and both smoking. Monsieur did all in his power to draw his phlegmatic fellow-passenger into conversation, but to no purpose. At last, with a superabundance of politeness, he apologised for drawing his attention to the fact that the ash of his cigar had fallen on his waistcoat, and that a spark was endangering his neckerchief.

The Englishman, now thoroughly aroused, exclaimed, "Why the devil can't you let me alone? Your coat-tail has been on fire for the last ten minutes, but I didn't bother you about it."

---

### SMOKING AT SCHOOL.

" OUR schoolmaster, who was an eccentric instructor, half Pestalozzi and half Philosopher Square, had an idea that all Spanish children were weaned upon tobacco, and absolutely permitted three Creole lads to smoke : on condition, however, that they should not light up their papelitos until night-time, when the other boys went to bed. How we used to envy them, as, marching in Indian file to our dormitories, we could see those favoured young Dons unrolling their squares of tissue-paper, preparatory to a descent into the play-ground and a quiet smoke ! The demoralisation among the juvenile community, caused by this concession to Spanish customs, was but slight. One or two of us tried surreptitious weeds on half-holiday afternoons; but the Widow Jones in Chiswick-lane did not keep quite such choice brands in stock as did Mr. Alcachofado, of the Morro Castle ; and Nemesis, in the shape of intolerable nausea, very soon overtook us. It is astounding, at fourteen years of age, how much agony of heart, brain, and stomach, can be got out of one penny Pickwick. Pestalozzi Square, Ph. Dr., very wisely refrained from excessive severity on this head. He made it publicly known that a boy detected in smoking would not necessarily be caned, but that on three alternate days for a week following the discovery of his offence, he would be supplied at 1 P.M. with a clean tobacco-pipe and half an ounce of prime shag, in lieu of dinner. We had very few unlicensed smokers after this announcement."

*G. A. Sala.*

---

### CARLYLE ON " THE VERACITIES."

ONE afternoon, when Carlyle's own stock of " free-smoking York River " had come to an end, and he had set out to walk with a friend, he stopped at a small tobacco-shop in Chelsea, facing the river, and went in to procure some temporary supply. The friend entered with him, and heard his dialogue with the shopkeeper. " York River " having been asked for, was duly produced; but, as it was not of the right sort, Carlyle, while making a small purchase, informed the shopkeeper most particularly what the right sort was, what was its name, and at what wholesale place in the City it might be ordered. " Oh ! we find that this suits our customers very well," said the man. "That may be, sir," said Carlyle, "but you will find it best in the long run always to deal in the veracities." The man's impression seemed to be that *the veracities* were some peculiar curly species of tobacco, hitherto unknown to him.

---

### CHILDREN'S PIPES.

IT was the custom in England, about the middle of the seventeenth century, for children going to school to carry in their satchel with their books a pipe of tobacco, which their mother took care to fill early in the morning, it serving them instead of a breakfast. At the accustomed hour every one laid aside his book to light his pipe, the master smoking with them, and teaching them how to hold their pipes and draw in the tobacco; thus using them to it from their youth, as a practice absolutely necessary for a man's health. At the present day, indeed, the Dutch children smoke pipes, and little boys of five and seven years old calmly discuss these calumets of peace as they proceed to school. The privation of tobacco is one of the weightiest punishments in the Dutch juvenile penal code.

### THE USES OF CIGAR ASH.

CIGAR ashes mingled with camphorated chalk make an excellent toothpowder; or, ground with poppy-oil, will afford for the use of the painter a varied series of delicate grays. Old Isaac Ostade so utilised the ashes of his pipe, but had he been aware of Havanas, he would have given us pictures even more pearly in tone than those which he has left for the astonishment and delight of mankind.

---

### AN INVETERATE SMOKER.

LOUIS PHILLIPPE'S principal gardener, "Père" Schoene, was one of those obstinate and self-willed mortals that disdain to yield to royalty itself. He was an inveterate smoker and was never seen without a pipe in his mouth. The king said to him one day, "It might be permitted for you to smoke before me, but to smoke thus before the queen and the princesses!"

"Sire," replied Schoene, "it is stronger than I am. If your majesty is discon-

tented with me, I will take my dismissal.
I shall die, perhaps, of chagrin, but it will
be with my pipe between my teeth."

The king smiled and forgave him.

---

## A TOUGH YARN.

AN amusing story is related by Commodore Wilkes in his "Narrative
of the United States Exploring Expedi-
tion." A native of the Feejee Islands
told him that a ship, the hull of which
was still lying on the beach, had come
ashore in a storm, and that the crew had
fallen into the hands of the cannibals.
"What did you do with them?" asked
Wilkes. "Killed them all," answered the
savage. "What did you do with them
after you had killed them?" was the next
question. "Eat 'em—good!" said the
Feejee, grinning. The Commodore felt
a qualm, as he inquired, faintly, "Did
you eat them all?" "Yes, we eat all
but one." "And why did you spare that
one?" asked Wilkes. "Because he taste
too much like tobacco; could'nt eat him
nohow."

### SOME FRENCH SMOKERS.

WHEN Dickens was in Paris he met the famous Madame Dudevant, better known as George Sand, who used to make, and of course smoke, her own cigars.    Girardin gave a banquet in honour of the brilliant English novelist, who in a letter related the following : "After dinner, Girardin asked me if I would come into another room and smoke a cigar ?   On my saying 'yes,' he coolly opened a drawer, containing about 5,000 inestimable cigars in prodigious bundles, —just as the captain of the robbers in ' Ali Baba ' might have gone to the corner of the cave for bales of brocade."   His wife, Madame de Girardin, has been credited with the saying, that " If Prometheus had stolen fire from heaven to light his cigar with, the gods would have suffered him to do it."   In France the pipe, which contemporaneously with the rise of German romanticism, renewed a popularity it still enjoys, has been consecrated by some of the prettiest sonnets in the language ; and the influence it exercises over some of the authors of these sonnets may be gathered from the concluding lines of one of the most

melodious of the poetical effusions of
Alphonse Karr :

"Il n'est pas de malheur qui surpasse ma peine :
  On m'a cassé ma pipe, il me reste à mourir."

In the Quartier Latin, the pipe has ever
been the great consoler in the bachelor
homes of Bohemian artists, and has even
usurped the sway of woman, as in the
case of the artist, Gavarni, who on his
death-bed is reported to have said to a
friend, "I leave you my wife and my pipe;
take care of my pipe."

---

### RIDDLES FOR SMOKERS.

A LITTLE book entitled, "The True
Trial of understanding, or Wit newly
revived," which was much hawked about
the country by chapmen in the reign of
Queen Anne, contains the following riddle:

"What tho' 1 have a nauseous breath,
    Yet many a one will me commend ;
I am beloved after death,
    And serviceable to my friend,"

to which is appended the answer, "This
is tobacco after cut and dry'd, being dead
becometh serviceable." The following
"quaint conceit" is still more clever.

To three-fourths of a cross add a circle complete :   TO
Let two semicircles a perpendicular meet :            B
Next add a triangle that stands on two feet:          A
Then two semicircles, and a circle complete :         CCO

## CIGAR MANUFACTURING IN HAVANA.

A CORRESPONDENT of the *New York Sun*, writing from Havana, gives the following account of one of the large cigar-manufacturing establishments there. He states that upon entering the factory, one is at once struck by the admirable coolness and ventilation of the place. On the ground floor, is a long warehouse, where the tobacco is stored. The tobacco used is of the crop of 1879, and, as the present crop is almost an entire failure, the manufacturers are making only enough cigars to fill their orders. They prefer to keep as much on hand as possible, expecting higher prices very soon. The average value of a bale of tobacco is about 75 dollars. Some of the very finest kinds of wrappings cost as much as 400 dollars a bale. Insurance is very high, the rate being one and a half per cent. upon the stock at the factory, and one per cent. upon that warehoused. At some factories the rate is even higher, on account of the wooden linings of the buildings. When the tobacco is taken from the bales it is distributed to the strippers, who take the bundles, sort them, stretch the leaves, remove the strong fibre that runs down the

middle of the leaf, and place the leaves
that are to serve as wrappers upon one
side. For this work they receive ten cents
gold for every ten carats. The pieces of
leaf that are too small for wrappers are then
carried up to the second floor where they
are spread out and separated into five
classes, according to the strength of the
flavour and the fineness of the leaf. Five
shafts run down to the floor beneath, and
each shaft is fed with tobacco of a different
class. These shafts deposit the tobacco
in the room where the cigar-makers
are at work, and each man, when
he wants more tobacco, takes a square
piece of canvass about the size of a large
pocket-handkerchief to the attendant, who
fills it from the proper shaft. Meantime
the wrappers are handed over to skilled
operators, who carefully sort them according to their fineness and colour. This is
the most important part of the whole process, as the profits of cigar-making depend
upon the nice judgment shown by the men
who separate the wrappers, and who give
the cigar-makers the kind suited to their
fillings. Should a fine wrapper be used
for an inferior cigar it would be clear waste,
and if a fine cigar be wrapped in a rough
leaf it would be thrown out by the man
who separates them. The room in which

the cigars are made is a large lofty apartment, with a stone floor. The cigarmakers sit in rows at benches, which are divided off by low partitions, to prevent the tobacco or cigars of two adjoining makers becoming mixed. A little hardwood board lies on the bench. Upon this the cigars are rolled. The cigarmaker takes from his heap of fillings enough tobacco to make a cigar. This, after placing in the binder, he fashions into shape, and then, taking a leaf from his heap of wrappers, folds carefully, trimming it with a sharp knife, and cutting it square off at the open end. Then he takes a small quantity of paste, smears it on the wrapper, and closes the smaller end of the cigar. Many cigar-makers give the end a twist in their mouths, and this is especially the case with the negroes engaged in this department. Each operator has a little mould, marked with the size of the cigar that he is making, and the cigar must measure exactly the proper length marked on the mould, and must pass through a hole bored in it. As soon as fifty cigars are finished they are tied in a bundle, and a slip of paper marked with the number of the maker is stuck under the string. When the time for paying comes the proprietor goes over these bundles, and pays so much per thousand for all the cigars made. The rate per thousand varies according to the size of the cigars and the excellence of the leaf. The best workmen are employed on the very finest kinds. The rough and cheap kinds are much more easy to make, and a good workman can turn out over two hundred cigars in eight hours. White men, negroes, and coolies are employed in cigar-making; but white labour is found to be by far the most intelligent, and coolie labour the least so. Indeed, the coolies are mostly employed in opening the bundles and separating the fillings from the wrappers, and very few of them are allowed to roll cigars. The cigar-makers—at least, the white ones—are a thriftless, lazy set. A folder will work until he has enough money for his immediate wants, and then he will at once leave his work until he is driven back penniless. One young, good-looking folder, engaged in making the best kinds of cigars, was pointed out by the proprietor as a curious example of this want of application. He works hard during five days of the week, making a tidy sum of money. Every Saturday night he visits a ready-made clothes-shop, buys a new suit, and early on Sunday goes either to the sea-shore or to the river, strips, bathes, and on coming out,

G

puts on his new suit.  Leaving the old one bought on the previous week, on the bank, he goes on the " spree," which lasts until his money is all spent, when he returns to work.  Women are also employed in sorting tobacco, but they are in a separate building, as it was found that the co-education of the sexes does not work so well in a Cuban cigar factory as in the æsthetic atmosphere of a New England College. They are of all colours, ranging from a pure white through every variety of cream and chocolate, up to a shining black that leaves Day and Martin's best efforts in the shade.  They all smoke, generally the very strongest cigars.  Unlike the clerk in the candy store, who is allowed to gorge himself at first, and who never cares for the sweet treasures again, men and women in tobacco factories do not lose their taste for smoking.  The manufacturers forbid smoking during work-hours, for it distracts the attention, and the cigars are less carefully made.  But the supply of cigars is almost unlimited, and every workman is allowed to carry away two or three. These cigars are made by boys who are only beginning, and whose productions are not good enough for market.  When the cigars are counted and the makers paid, the former are sent upstairs and carefully

sorted, first to remove the badly made
ones and those with rough wrappers, and
then to divide them, according to the
colour of the leaf, into colorados and
maduros. When this is done, they are
ready to be placed in boxes which are
made in a separate part of the factory.
The boxes when filled are placed under a
press, and the cigar is then ready for sale.
So great is the demand for cigars, that one
factory, although turning out 45,000 a day,
is soon to be enlarged, and it is expected
that when this is done, 60,000 cigars a day
will be made. At the present moment
none of the well-known factories have
more than fifty or one hundred boxes of
cigars on hand, over and above the amount
required to fill their orders. This is partly
owing to the reluctance of cigar manufacturers to use up the crop of 1879 until a
rise in prices makes a larger profit. It re-
quires at least three days to make a cigar
from the time the tobacco is taken out of
the bale. The first day is spent in soak-
ing the bunches, the second in picking and
folding, and on the third the cigar is ready
to be placed in the boxes. But it is usual
to allow a longer time to elapse, so that
the cigars may not be too fresh when packed.
The refuse tobacco, too small for fillings,
is sent to the cigarette manufactory, which

belongs, as a rule, to the same proprietor, or is sold to snuff-makers. This is the ordinary process of manufacture in Havana; but each *fabrica* differs in some trifling way from the others. The wages paid are also slightly different, according to the style and quality of the goods manufactured. But the system is the same throughout. In buying cigars the first thing to do is to find out what factory has bought the best tobacco of the year, and then to procure the cigars made altogether of that crop, and not mixed with the inferior tobacco of some other year. The lands where the best plants used to grow are becoming worn out, and planters use guano manure. The tobacco grown in this way has not the fine flavour or aroma that the product of the same land had in former years.

Printed in the United States
76188LV00001B/49

9 781410 102706